God Is a Woman
The Path to *Singlediversity*

by

Edin Husković

Translated from the Bosnian language by the GIAW team, Mostar

For permission, serialization, condensation, adaptations, or for our catalog of other publications, write to Ozark Mountain Publishing, Inc., P.O. Box 754, Huntsville, AR 72740, ATTN: Permissions Department.

Library of Congress Cataloging-in-Publication Data

God is a Woman
by Edin Husković -1973-

This book will, consequently, primarily deal with raising awareness of its reader. If we only manage to raise awareness in every man, the man will open the doors slightly towards the area of his own changes for the better.

1. Self-Help 2. Metaphysical 3. Self-Awareness
I. Husković, Edin -1973- II. Self-Help III. Metaphysical IV. Title
Library of Congress Catalog Card Number: 2023933151
ISBN: 978-1-950639-18-2

Cover Art and Layout: Victoria Cooper Art
Book set in: Times New Roman, Segoe Script, Nelson Ornaments
Book Design: Summer Garr
Published by:

PO Box 754, Huntsville, AR 72740
800-935-0045 or 479-738-2348; fax 479-738-2448
WWW.OZARKMT.COM

Printed in the United States of America

Contents

Part 1

The Metaphor of My Life

Among the various things with which I have been occupied is owning and operating a small gift store in the city of Mostar, Bosnia-Herzegovina. I've had *quite a struggle*. Running a store can be decent work. However, any work will lose its charm when it fails to function as expected. One can only imagine that few global economic pursuits could succeed if they were given the situation in this town, region, country, and part of the continent. Although I should not use it as an excuse, this certainty alleviates the misery in my soul caused by my own failures.

Opening the gift store would not have been such a poor business move had I not incurred some previous debts, a number of unmet claims, and three or four bank loans (massive recession of 2008 to today). People openly speak about our national debt of millions in US dollars. My private budget has been one of those that felt the impact of such an unfavorable general business climate—and no wonder.

But, there is no way I will give up this time. It would be stupid, impractical, and unprofitable. Simply said, I would deprive myself of my daily bread. As such, giving up is not an option, especially for one who has a three-year-old boy to look after. Therefore, I have come to the conclusion that I should *grit my teeth*, take one more bank loan if necessary, unblock my currently blocked bank account, and thus prepare for the upcoming tourist season. I am writing this in mid-May and, if nothing else, Mostar has become a summer holiday destination for thousands of domestic

3

and foreign tourists who come to see the Old Bridge, built of stone in 1566 during Ottoman rule and now on UNESCO's World Heritage List.

My gift store has also become a popular destination along with the old section of Mostar; the Catholic pilgrimage site in Međugorje; the famous Tekke, a monastery for the Islamic Dervish order at the source of the Buna River; the Orthodox monastery in Žitomislići, and many other natural and cultural sights in Herzegovina.

Summer brings about changes, movement, and economic prosperity, and eventually our community ceases to be the hidebound, backwater town where we live the rest of the year. But, until the change occurs, one finds oneself already in debt, nerves shattered, chronically exhausted, severely depressed, and hardly capable of living through the day. From the time one rises in the morning until late in the evening when one retires, he is painfully aware of the restless night, of the nightmares and sweating that await.

As a matter of fact, an event which is perfect for the metaphor of my life took place today.

I wanted to do something nice for my family and myself, maybe even something symbolic. I bought a twenty-five-liter aquarium intending to create a small lush environment for fish and plants. A friend of mine decided to close his pet shop in the vicinity of my store. This was a great opportunity to buy a glass aquarium, lake sand, several warm-water fish, and four or five types of aquatic plants for minimum cost. So I did it. I figured out where to put my aquarium. Then I rushed home to tidy up our small flat so that I could set it up. This was a surprise for my son and for my girlfriend, who was supposed to pick him up from kindergarten on her way back from work. When one is upset by a life of hardship, feeling distant or embarrassed for whatever reason, it's fun to gaze at colorful fish swimming in an aquarium. Each one of them living in their own world is also together with the other fish as part of a small habitat you yourself have created to some extent. It can be quite relaxing. You simply get carried away.

I put the aquarium on the chest of drawers in the living room and filled it with water. Soon after, not straight away, but some ten or fifteen minutes after I poured all the water, I heard dripping:

drip, drip, drip … Apparently, while I was pouring the water into the aquarium, it was leaking quite badly on the other side. Later, I realized that the water was coming from the seam between the two glass sides facing the wall. It was caused, I suppose, by failure in the sealant when the aquarium was made. First, water covered the chest of drawers' surface and then it started leaking down the backside onto the parquet floor. It took me fifteen minutes to notice it. By then water covered almost one-fifth of the floor. Thinking about a hose in the yard and the physical law of connected vessels, I barely managed to collect all the water. Instead of the nice atmosphere I was hoping to create for us all, I caused damage. It was definitely the last thing I could think of in that context.

Well, that pretty much sums up my life. Whatever I have done so far, it has never come out well. As they say, "If something can go wrong, it will." All the works I have started ended like that— my personal plans and all other decisions I have made. There is always an obstacle ahead, a leakage, a crack, or a gap, that I am not aware of. I usually have no idea when, why, or how it happens.

A Message in the Bottle

I have thought about God and the true meaning of life ever since I was a child. I was born in a Muslim family during the communist-socialist era of the former Yugoslavia. My granny, on Mum's side, had some knowledge of religion; people say she knew the *Holy Quran* by heart. She passed away when I was two and half years old so I don't really have memories of her. All I remember is her room upstairs and her prayer rug. In that room, where she spent most of her time, there was a two-seater settee that turned into a bed, a small chest of drawers with the *Holy Quran* on the top shelf, her prayer rug, and prayer beads.

People say that after playing with me once, she said, in low tones, "My little grandson Edo's thoughts are all over the place." I believe I have never been so insightfully perceived. Hundreds and thousands of the most disconnected thoughts are continuously going through my mind, never allowing me peace. I am also prone to negative autosuggestion, giving myself unpleasant ideas, which enhances anxious and depressive mental crises. I find these mental crises devastating at times. At other times I manage to overcome them. I struggle with nerves just as other people struggle with cardiovascular problems and chronic hepatitis. I always worry that my health will fail. I am a coward, though I have been trying to be braver.

When I sometimes manage to achieve a state of *detachment*, it comes as a relief and brings me a step toward more positive thinking and *feeling better about my life*. Then I begin functioning. I write, eat (a lot), ride my bike, listen to music and radio, watch

TV, play with my son, kiss my girlfriend, tidy up our place, vacuum, go someplace in the car, invite friends for a cup of coffee. And they invite me, too. I read, learn, and think a lot about the meaning and purpose of life, which in my case seems to be incoherent and empty.

I will try to be more specific: There is not enough life in my life even though I have been trying frantically to change that. I love life and believe I should take much more of it than it seems to offer, at least than it is offering me.

In order to find some logic in my existence, lately, I have been more and more reliant on conversations with myself.

Do you ever talk to yourself? Do you ever ask yourself questions and try to get answers? Do you ever get an impression that there is some other you, an intuitive you, more you than you. Whatever you call it, there is a higher form of yourself that remains intact at all times, whether it is favorable to you, is on your side, or not. Despite what my granny said, part of my mind remains unchanged while the rest keeps changing form, transforming in different ways. Sometimes those directions are good; sometimes, not so good.

Lately, that other, unchanged and quiet part of my mind has been in touch with my conscious mind. Call it my higher self.

I ask my higher self for answers to agonizing questions that will make sense of my life. As I have been looking for spiritual truths, I have discovered my universal me. It existed in me before, but I was not aware of it.

I remember the beginnings of my search when I would ask, "Mum, does God exist?" I think that my mother, Fikreta, did not bother much with this question of mine. She would answer only, "Sure he does." I would continue, "Has anyone ever seen God?" Mum wouldn't then know exactly what she was supposed to say, so she would answer, "Muhammad is a prophet of God." But I persisted, "What is a prophet of God? Did Muhammad see God?" "A prophet is the one sent by Allah for mankind. Granny used to say that the sky opened above Muhammad, and he then stood before God."

One such conversation took place when Bosnian Muslims were celebrating the twenty-seventh night of Ramadan, Laylatul Qadr. According to a religious legend, exactly at midnight on Laylatul Qadr, when we remember the prophet's assumption, the sky opens above all good Muslims. It would of course be impossible for common people to ascend to heaven as Allah favored the prophet. Nevertheless, through an opening in the sky angels fulfill all the good people's wishes. I spent one such summer night in the courtyard, looking at a clear sky full of stars (and a Mahala would jokingly add, "*and a few moons*"). I was waiting for the sky to open and angels to appear. I fell asleep on a couch sometime before dawn, having failed to experience what I had hoped for. Not for one moment during the whole night did the dark sky full of stars open or any angels appear.

When I woke up, I came to the following conclusions. The first was that I understood *God will never like me as much as he likes Muhammad so I stand no chances of reaching him in the sky.* The second one was more discouraging, even devastating: *I am not a good Muslim, and not a good boy, since no angels spoke to me last night when they came to all good children, and to men and women who waited for them in contrition.*

Being a ten-year-old at the time, I thought there was no place for me under God's sky or with good people. These conclusions were quite depressing, and, not surprisingly, I became an atheist. It relieved my pressured mind, and, besides, our socialist educational system supported atheism.

The next conclusion was: *there are neither Gods nor angels. The explanations for various natural phenomena, and the reason we exist and act throughout the centuries, have been ascribed to divinities, or to only one. As a result, various religions and beliefs in magic were devised, because we lacked a better explanation.*

Anyway, I did not like the idea of a horrible and righteous God; a God who punishes; a God who has no mercy toward the godless; a God who under certain circumstances will not hesitate to put you through hell. God had his favorites: righteous Muslims. He cursed others: those who never addressed him or didn't approach him in the proper way. God had his needs in relation to us, or in the best case, he had no needs with regards to those he created. However, if we failed to address him as strictly and precisely defined by a code of behavior, he would put us in the terrible pain of eternal fire.

I was afraid of such a God, so I replaced my fear with another, more comforting thought. There is no God. We should rely on human kindness and all the gifts that nature herself gives us spontaneously.

But deep in my heart I felt that I had it wrong, that all my conclusions were illogical and inconsistent with the beauty of truth. It may have been true that there was no oppressive, vindictive, only conditionally merciful God. However, if there were no such God, but there were a different, more helpful God, would atheism still make sense?

But what if God is not the opposite of what he is supposed to be? I kept asking questions deep in my heart trying to get answers and find conclusions. What if there is a God and he is not Absolute prone to punish? Then, he should be a God of love, forgiveness, acceptance, gentleness, and good intentions. But then again, assuming this is true, why are we surrounded with imperfection, suffering, disharmony, natural disasters, war, disease, and death? A perfect, merciful God would be opposed to the imperfect world which he created. For many years after I was a ten-year-old boy who waited for the sky to open up, it was hard for me to understand and explain those contradictions.

Until this very day, for me the mystery of living and its purpose remains too distant and complex, even though the voice of an inner universal or higher me is clearer, is submissive and determined more than ever to resolve these questions.

I weigh 116 kg—maybe even a few kilos more. I have lived through war, poverty, and destruction. I have faced fears that I am not ready to write about now. I failed to create the life for my girlfriend that she wanted. I am skeptical about a better future for my child. I live in an uncertain postwar stalemate, in debt up to my neck, and my current business prospects are not promising.

How could anyone remain positive under such negative circumstances as these?

What follows is the start of my conversation with God as I sought the answers to these questions.

First of all: Peace and Love!

Hmm … Hello, God Almighty. It is not you that I have heard this greeting "Peace and Love" from. A friend of mine, Dragan Hadrović, has been using it for some time.

Yes, child. I inspired Dragan Hadrović to use that greeting, starting quite some time ago. It is a good one. On the other hand, today is your first significant attempt at writing down the dialogue you will be having with your universal self.

I tried to do it once, before even the notion of *Diary from the Stomach* came to me and turned into a book. But I was afraid that transcribing an exchange with you would be a poor copy of *Conversations with God* that Neale Donald Walsch wrote.

I believe you failed to record our conversation because you did not believe that it was possible.

Well, yes! I am not sure that I know what I am doing even now as I start. What will a dialogue with my universal me sound like? What will inspire me?

Nevertheless, you clearly feel that it is likely to be an interesting writing experience, and that it will take you places you have never been or dreamt about. You will *raise* yourself.

My universal me seems to be unexpectedly outside myself. It is as though a conversation has started between two different people. This is not what I initially thought it would be. I rather hoped to talk with a subconscious part of myself, instead.

You need two people to have a dialogue. Otherwise, it is a monologue. Obviously, from the very beginning, you have been inspired by one thought only: to have a dialogue in writing. For the time being, we shall not get into a dilemma about whether your universal you is a completely separate entity which is by your side, and not some part of you which together with your conscious part makes a complete unit. At the very beginning I must tell you something very important: *As with all other dilemmas, the truth is somewhere in between.*

Therefore, it is very much possible that I am not having this dialogue with myself but with a completely separate and independent entity who resides with me in my body and my mind.

Yes, maybe that's just about it—and maybe it's not. As I said, speaking as a woman, the truth is usually between the two opposite possibilities. But, it is not so important now. Let's let

the dialogue continue.

You spoke as a man. You spoke as a woman. As a woman! Oh, don't tell me that my universal me is female. Am I talking to some universal woman by my side or one who is inseparable from me?

Now we have two dilemmas and two possibilities: The one with whom you are talking—am I an inseparable hyperinternal part of you or not? Or are you talking to a completely different person?

And the second question is even more intriguing: Is the other party to this strange communication male or female if I am, indeed, separate from you?

This idea suggests an incredible possibility!

I know.

You know.

Of course.

Well, is it true?

I need you to ask me a concrete and complete question.

And you know the answer?

Of course, but I don't want you to avoid formulating a question.

I will have to ask it, and it will have to be complete and concrete.

Don't hesitate. I am blissfully waiting to hear it.

Well, all right. Is it possible that what I have thought to be my universal me is, in fact, a separate part of me, an individual expanded throughout existence, both material and spiritual creation? Is it what some teachings call Paramatma, Supreme Soul, a localized aspect of God present in every atom of the created, but still part of one, personal God?

And ...

And ... is that aspect—a woman? Woman—God?

And you are expecting an answer to your questions now?

Surely!

A true answer.

Why are you procrastinating? I've done my part and asked indicative questions.

Magnificent questions. Magnificent questions, my dear.

Are they really?

It is not that you are immodest because you are not me, and I am not you even though we have been the inseparable One for eons. You have to understand that.

 No, it is not at all about the fact that you will disregard modesty. It is me who is going to say this: these are the most magnificent questions that a human being can ask himself, other human beings, or me. Questions: Am I personal and am I a woman? In the end, being such male or female, am I talking to you from your deepest part of you? Magnificent questions, my dear!

And I am waiting for responses.

The answer is in a bottle.

What is this now—a joke? Are you dodging something?

Both your magnificent questions and my witty remark reflect one universal truth.

And I am waiting to hear it. I am eager to hear it.

I have already said it. I have already responded to your questions before you even asked them.

So, where are the answers? What bottle?!

Yes and it reads: *As with all other dilemmas, the truth is somewhere in between.*

 Well, I am a part of you which is you, but I am also a completely separate part from you. I am a woman, but I am also a man, because there is nothing that I am not or can't

be. I am truth, light, and inspiration. And yes, if you want, all answers were in the bottle. The bottle hid answers to all your questions, just as is the case with all other questions you will or have ever wanted to ask. As for many questions, so for many answers, and each answer will require only one thing from you: Break every bottle ahead on your way. The sooner and more consistently you break it, the clearer and more magnificent answer you will get. Just as with the questions you will ask me, regardless of what they refer to, and how bizarre they may sound at first. Therefore, ask questions, even those seemingly bizarre questions. Some answers will be hidden in bizarreness, including the most important and most magnificent answers that will knock you off your feet. But from your unstable posture you can reach the highest level of thought about yourself or any person who has been, in one way or another, part of your life.

This book will gain significance, because now is an era of awakening, a renaissance, the time you have been waiting for. Seize the chance and make the best out of it.

I am a kind lady and I never prevent possibilities from coming. I always recreate life conditions offering new chances, and once you use one of these opportunities I keep providing for you, the first truth to burst out in front of your eyes will be the following: *Each answer you are really looking for is in the bottle. Break it and benefit from what has been given to you.*

The truth is in breaking open, breaking every misconception and illusion, error, stereotype, or dogma, bad tradition, cultural misconception, religious dogma, or personal intention.

The truth is an explosion.

The truth is the explosion of your astonished humility at the beauty and rarity of the Absolute. At this point humility turns into true power.

It has been quite some time since the most unusual and sublime truths came to this planet: I am a Kind Woman, Blessed Lady, Dark Skin Dancer, Unruly Woman, Skillful Horsewoman, Beautiful Face, Trickster, Dazzling Dancer, Everlasting Benefactor. I am God and Goddess. I am who I Am, who I Was, and who I Will Be. There is nothing without me, I am outside of everything.

That's it. One of the bottles has broken. The truth leaked out.

I am the Alpha and the Omega, the beginning and the end, all the truths are in me, and I am in them.

I am an endless expansion, matter and antimatter, the essential element of all material worlds and transcendental creation.

And as long as you breathe, drink water, eat to strengthen, as long as you witness the constant changes and most diverse fantastic aspects of life, of which you are an inseparable part, as long as you step on this soil, I will share with you every drop of water, atom of the air, and morsel.

I am your most sublime inspiring thought leading ahead.

I am your God.

I am your wife.

Amen.

Tá Hâ

You are my wife?

Yes.

I don't understand. It sounds great, but I don't understand.

It did not jar your hearing when I said I am your God?

Why would it? That statement is recognizable. You are not only my God, but also the God of all people, if it is God that I am talking to right now. But I have never heard of God as someone's wife. I am embarrassed by that supposition, to say the least.

If you deny that God may be a wife to you, then you deny the absolute nature of God. You deny the obvious, simple truth. All truths are simple. I am God that I am. I am everything and everything is in me. There is nothing that I am not, there has never been anything that wasn't me, nor will it be through eternity. I say, "I am everything that exists!" Is it possible then that anything that is, is not me? Among the infinite possibilities stretching endlessly in all directions, am I not or cannot I be female?

<u>Whoever denies any aspect of my personality actually denies me in an entirety.</u>

Here is a useful question: What relation can you have with me as your wife?

Okay, what kind of relation *can* I have with you as my wife?

Unconditional love. If the question is what relation can you have with me as your God, the answer is the same. The answer is always the same. Unconditional love is our common destiny. What is the problem then if I say, "In addition to everything else, God is also a perfect wife?"

Now I see, I don't have a problem with it.

You think it is not a problem for you.

I think it's not. Should it be?

The way you see it—not anymore.

So, where's the catch?

In resistance.

Resistance?

Release *GOD IS A WOMAN* into the ether, and you have made a more dynamic and *dangerous statement* than you realize. If someone had dared to say that in the Middle Ages in Europe, he would have been burned at the stake. Now, try to go to Tehran or Riyadh and shout that Allah is a woman and you would be stoned with more zeal and intoxication than was ever hurled at a prostitute, or rather a woman declared to be a prostitute. Western intellectuals will laugh in your face. Many will run away from your book as soon as they spot the title. People will single you out, make fun of you, and do whatever it takes to separate you from that impossible statement: GOD IS A WOMAN—to your circulating that blasphemous idea. Mosques will be shaking, church towers tilting, and synagogues trembling to the foundations. GOD IS FEMALE! GOD IS FEMALE! Deadly conspiracies will be organized against you. You will be a target.

So are you ready to be a great cavalier? Are you prepared to sacrifice your comfort, forget about your physical safety, and persist in such a dangerous mission and do all of it only for me? Will you be prepared to sacrifice yourself for one of my kisses, a private letter, or statement of love? Will you suffer, struggle, and anguish for a woman, only one woman?

I think you know me very well.

I know you very well, not just sufficiently, and not just well. I know what your reaction would be in this case.

Then you know my answer.

I do! The answer is in the bottle.

Help me break it …

Tá Hâ.

From Suicide to God

It may sound strange or irresponsible, but at this point I am not disturbed by the consequences if I declare that God is female.

Other issues worry you.

Yes.

Talk about them. Write something. Take a critical look at your daily routine. Detect all your problems. Clearly and fully.

That's an order.

I never *give orders*. Not to you, not now, not to anyone, not at any times. I suggest. I advise, respond to your prayers, and deliberately lead you to certain conclusions. *Sometimes it happens that I say things about the future in the form of a present statement. It may seem to be an order, but it's not.*

I never make anyone do anything in order to satisfy my will. On the contrary, your will is an order for me.

I have created a universe that will fulfill your every desire. It is not some forced kindness, but a consequence of my endless and unconditional love for everyone and everything. It is unfortunate when you overlook the gifts that I have made available to you. It is your problem when you deny the enormous power I have given you.

You deprive yourself of yourself. You exist incompletely, in a permanent and agonizing half life, ignoring countless

messages that point toward what you really are and what you can make of yourself. **Self-realization is your destiny, just as much as it is the destiny of all human beings on your planet.**

Self-realization means knowledge; knowledge sets the truth free; truth reveals the power of your being, the magnificence of your spirit, the abilities of your mind, and your corporal function. You are not your body. Nevertheless, your flesh is an important, an inevitable factor of what you are while you are inhabiting it.

As if you are suggesting an answer even before I have asked a question …

Which implies I have never ordered you to do anything. So I repeat: Sometimes it happens that I say things about the future in a form of a present statement. It may seem to be an order, but it's not. I knew then everything about your decision referring to the near future so I just encouraged you: Face the reality. Straight away and to the fullest.

How can I live with your knowing what is going to happen in my future, especially when you know the future will be awful, and yet you don't do anything about it?

I can and will act as an advisor. My message is clear. Take into account that my suggestions in the present will never lead you off the right path in the future.

Each act of mine endangering the respect of your free will to do with yourself and in yourself whatever you like would annul the basic rules regulating the perfection of the relation between me and you and these rules include freedom and independence.

On the other hand, good and bad are relative notions. *Things are never so bad that they can't be made good in the end. Besides, there is no guarantee that what we consider good will not eventually turn bad.* **Thus, you find it tough to judge whether an experience is good or bad. Or to sum it**

up: *Everything is absolutely good, because both good or bad things are part of a process leading to perfection and entirety. It's a metaphysical truth and now we are moving toward a practical level.*

Yes! Even before I asked a question, you gave me an answer. My next questions will follow statements that offer clarification. May I start?

Certainly! That's what we are here for.

Well, here we go. I will try to give a short but meaningful description of my day. I wake up in the morning tired and exhausted. Almost immediately, I lie down again on the sofa in the living room. I feel as if I did not sleep at all or that the time I slept did not serve its purpose. I am exhausted and tired all the time. Each new day arrives overshadowed by old concerns: lack of money to pay bills on time, poor health, irritability, and relentless depression with devastating anxiety. I don't want to play with my own child or be a partner to my girlfriend. Yet, with all my might I try to restore beauty in my relationship with my girlfriend. I try to play with my son.

Fear. Fear of today, fear of tomorrow, terror when I remember past troubles. Fear of various diseases. Fear of myself, fear of something which I can't name, and fear of fear. Fear that comes with the conviction that prayer is pointless, that God is remote. I feel my own alienation, am anxious that I cannot change things for the better.

Morning television is bizarre: foreign policy, domestic dilemmas, ethnic and religious intolerance. Music is horrible, the so-called turbo-folk music.[1] Children's TV shows are stupid and meaningless. Cooking shows in diverse TV kitchens lead into electoral competition and governmental crises. The economy slides into debt and insolvency. Unemployment is up. All of the aforementioned lead to the creation of lethargic masses and disinterested individuals.

An independent archaeologist, Semir Osmanagić, claims to have discovered pyramids in central Bosnia. I wish he did.

---

1   Turbo-folk: naćinaInternetu.

Certain domestic experts and politicians have been trying to deny Osmanagić's thesis even before he has tried to prove it. I can't stand experts and journalists who tend to stagnate; sensation is what we need; we cry out for movement; changes are necessary. My girlfriend and I need one more loan to buy new inventory for the shop. At the same time, we are uneasy about the possibility of bankruptcy. I talked to a man I talked to yesterday; I talked to another man I talked to yesterday and the day before yesterday; surely, I talked to the first man the day before yesterday; with both of them I talked about topics we tackled both yesterday and the day before yesterday or some other day in the past.

During the day I work; I can't fall asleep until late, and when I manage to, I am scared by nightmares. I wake up the next morning drowsy and exhausted. As we endure these problems, how can I explain to her that despite all, God is with us?

You can do it once you persuade yourself that God is with you. In fact, you do know it, but you don't know that you know. Knowledge consists of harmonizing truth, which is deep in you, with real life as you experience it. It will bring you close to wisdom.

Wisdom is applied knowledge. Knowledge unapplied is almost the same as ignorance. Therefore, any appropriate answer, be it even metaphysical and abstract, must be embodied into your own reality, in all of your choices.

How can I apply knowledge in my own life and thus reach wisdom?

There are three levels of belief that experience will bring you. First, hope is awakened. If you pray, in whatever way, hope will be your first step toward wisdom. Prayers mixed with hope are one way. You may address me unaware that I can and want to address you, too.

Sooner or later, hope turns into belief in a particular outcome. Things do not always turn out the way you hoped for, but they quite often do if you have faith. Even at this stage, people may experience "broken faith." Their knowledge and assumptions about their circumstances surpass both the persistence of their hope and the intensity of their belief.

When it comes to a particular outcome that you desire,

there is no place for uncertainty, loss of hope, or lack of faith. The amount of knowledge is proportionate to the amount of desired outcome. If you achieve a goal, it implies you have acquired a thorough knowledge of the matter. PLEASE BE AWARE THAT I AM ALWAYS WITH YOU AND ANY REQUIREMENT WILL BE MET. For that reason the universe exists, planets move, stars shine; black holes appear and disappear, all in order for your wishes to come true—except for when you are ignorant that it is so. Such ignorance, all by itself, exhausts hope and invalidates belief. Ignorance pushes you down. Once the last ray of hope is destroyed, you are overwhelmed by despair—a constant and inevitable life of despair, which will lead to depression. Depression kills emotion, desire, volition. Depression disrupts life's rhythm. It makes nonexistence more attractive than life; at its rock bottom it leads to a suicide.

I have been noticing more and more depressed people. How come? How can it happen that you do not know something you know and then, urged by some side conditions, you decide when your life will stop? How can so much imperfection in the world survive while God is perfect?

Life is a process; life is constant change. Every moment is different from the one before. The change is a life prime mover. Agreeing to hit the bottom of life is basically the soul's cry for change. Spirit does not tolerate stagnation. Therefore, do not criticize the complex conditions in which you find yourself. Rather try to identify them as indicators that you need to change something. The more painfully and complex these indicators build up, the more determined you should be to act upon them. Try to regain hope, rely on your faith, and be aware, I repeat: BE AWARE that everything giving you a hard time and making you feel hopeless is a stimulus toward change. Realize that there is no insurmountable obstacle. Such knowledge will make you certain that there is no darkness you will not be able to see through and that any mistake you may make will eventually be forgiven.

And rely on another truth: No one can scare or hurt you so badly that you will not be able to recover. Such knowledge, in a larger sense, includes its three components: Certainty,

Reliance, and Doubtlessness. All of those are pillars of Absolute Knowledge. When you hit bottom and you wish you didn't exist, try not to criticize the condition. Don't you think that someone else but you put you in such a misery? Think of that problem as a powerful stimulus to your spirit (your deepest you). Use it for understanding and transformation. It can open the door to new ways of existence you have never thought of before.

Further, turn to me with Absolute Certainty, Reliance, and Doubtlessness to grasp the perfection of existence and turn from suicide to the channel of life that is open, happy, and exalting your God as I, as your God, will move the universe, stop the time for you, raise you up, or simply said, do anything to make you succeed.

From suicide to Gods?!

That's right, my dear! From suicides to Gods, the star-carrying Gods.

How I Told God a Joke

Before I get back to life skills, I would like to say a few words about the town I live in. From a literary point of view, it is good to intertwine topics and motives.

I agree. Mostar is the city of light.

Perhaps I see my city from a different angle.

It is great. We are One, but at the same time we are completely different. Being One does not necessarily mean being identical. I do not support any kind of uniformity. Being One and unique go hand in hand with making the phenomenon of life great and magnificent. To express one's personality, knowing how we are all One, that is wisdom brought to light. The hiding place of wisdom is in contradiction. We will discuss it later.
    Now, tell me something about your wonderful city.

Well, for me, my town is not so wonderful. Mostar is a city of losers, of presumptuous, arrogant people with low self-esteem. My street is full of such losers. I myself, being a hopeless case, still hold a high opinion of myself based on no grounds whatsoever. People believe that no strangers in Mostar should get smart with them. The truth is that even though a chance traveler may get the impression that Herzegovinians are clever, the locals create that impression through deceit or, worse, through a calculated cheap bluff. That's Mostarians.
    Common-sense principles in this place were lost a long time ago. At the beginning of the twenty-first century, there are

but one or two technologically advanced companies in Mostar. There are no pedestrian paths; cyclists are few; yet bars and gambling shops are overcrowded. Everyone here would like to be an innkeeper and thereby a master, a boss. Not even those few successful businessmen expect anything beyond the most primitive, constricted trade. And those who finish at celebrated schools, who talk about themselves as advanced, remain as weak in practice as they are strong in theory, regardless of their profession or sphere. Consequently, things usually don't go any further than making disorganized plans.

Nevertheless, people talk and lecture a lot. There is a joke about two Mostarians talking: The first says, "Have you heard of the death of that friend of mine?"

"He died!? What makes him believe he can die?!!!!" says the other, his eyes popping.

See, you don't have the right to die in this place. Forget finding work or making a living. Everything is miserable, everything is stupid, everything will fail except the opinions of some infallible critic.

People are envious and mutually destructive so that when a Mujo died and ended up in hell, he saw devils-guards around every hole except one. The head devil said they didn't need guards around that hole because "Mostarians are down there. If one of them tries to escape from hell, the rest will pull him back down." That's the way people are like here.

By contrast, our climate is generous and life giving, totally opposite to the people. God, I suppose you place good next to evil for balance. Days here are usually sunny and bright all year. Truth be told, winters are cold and blustery, and summers are swelteringly hot. But the light makes this place special— Mediterranean light. Ivo Andrić, one of our most famous national writers,[2] wrote that in the morning, it's not the sound that wakes you up in Mostar. It's the glorious light. He was right.

The old bridges, the towers, houses, and streets are made of a stone that gleams as it does in nature. Mediterranean flora, birds, and clouds, even cars, trucks, trailers, tires, PVC windows, wrought-iron grills and doors, windows of old houses, churches

---

2   Ivo Andrić, BiH writer and the Nobel Prize winner in Literature.

and mosques—everything gleams more translucently on a Mostar morning than in any other time or place in the world, with more energy than even you'll see thirty kilometers north of here.

Yet when you live in Mostar, you come under the constant scrutiny of gossipers and can be blinded by the too strong light of their judgment.

And the street on which you live is interesting, is it not?

Can you possibly be interested in the stupid, bizarre situation of our existence?

Well, there is one thing you should know: Nothing in the world is more or less valuable than something else. As their mother, I haven't created any human to be more or less worthy than others. From the position of Absolute Reality, I don't see any difference between a Sudanese woman with her two starving children at the foot of Kordofan and Jennifer Lopez, who is buying a fur coat in Beverly Hills at the same time.

From your point of view, the difference between these two souls may seem insurmountable, but from my perspective they have both chosen the places and living conditions that will take them to final enlightenment and Holy spirituality in the shortest possible time and in the most efficient manner. Both the desperate Sudanese with her *weakened* children and the rich and famous J. Lo are in the perfect circumstances to lead them to me, the Absolute. Their eternal home is not in the material world with its illusory suffering or happiness, with which you are in irregular touch.

So, there is no difference between me and you, or me and anyone else; we are all One, and all our diverse circumstances are temporary and transient.

Exactly. But remember not to mix up oneness and sameness. We are One, but we are different, and the main difference between me and you, and between any other spiritual personality and me, is not in quality but in quantity.

I don't understand.

I will try to simplify things. Try to follow me. The *anonymous*

Sudanese woman and *famous* Jennifer are One. Their apparent differences are temporary and transient, and are also perfect so that each of them can achieve her goals and fulfill her wishes.

And the supreme goal and most supreme wish for each of them and for you is to become aware of yourself. I am in the heart of all living creatures and so am I in the hearts of these two women. I perfectly know all the lives you lived before and I perfectly know the mysterious paths that each soul chooses in order to reach final realization of itself. What seems one person's wealth, beauty, and power, or another person's jeopardy, poverty, and misery is nothing but the perfect circumstances for finding complete fulfillment, in time, for each of them.

You may see your city and its residents in the same way. In each context, try to see its real cause. Otherwise, how can you understand wealth unless you have experienced poverty? How can you know what it means to be fed if you have not starved? You will be able to love splendor only if you have lived in darkness; there is no up without down. And so it goes down to the very last detail: HAVING A DIRECT EXPERIENCE OF ONE EXTREME UNFAILINGLY MAKES YOU UNDERSTAND ITS OPPOSITE. That is a great truth. And there are more TRUTHS I will ask you to accept: WE ARE ALL ONE. WE ARE ALL MADE OF ETERNAL SPIRITUAL SUBSTANCE: ME AS ENDLESS SPIRIT, EVERY ONE OF YOU AS ENDLESSLY SMALL SPIRITUAL PARTICLES. But the quality of transcendence, regardless of its size, is always the same. WE ARE ALL ONE, BUT WE ARE ALSO DIFFERENT. The overall beauty of existence lies in simultaneous oneness and diversity. THE TRUTH LIES IN CONTRADICTION.

I believe I am beginning to understand, but I will definitely be getting back to the previous part of this conversation in the future.

Or I will be repeating it for you in every other context. The most interesting stories are related to eternal truths. Truth permeates everything, just as it does in life. And we are all spiritual particles permeating an eternal and endless course of existence. Gojka Vukovića, the street where you live, is part of the magnificent process, one of its mysterious whirls. Your description of Mostar is uniquely yours and innate to you. I enjoy hearing it. I love the way you express yourself. How can you suppose that I wouldn't love something that is yours and someone such as you? How can you even think that I have a low opinion of you only because you are currently surrounded by circumstances you consider imperfect? My love for you is unconditional, and it can be no other way. Please understand it and accept it, because here's our opportunity for what stands ahead of us is an unusual experience of reintroduction, understanding, and mutual love. Our love is starting to burn again. Let's give way to our feelings. Don't even think that I will ever sing "I Don't Want You to Walk down My Street,"[3] as the song goes.

There is, then, a universe; there is a galaxy in that universe; somewhere, at the bottom of spirally placed constellations, there is a solar system and a planet in it. There are seven continents on that planet. On one of them, there is a particular country. In that country, there is a city among others. And in that city, one neighborhood: DONJA MAHALA.

Nobody knows how it got its name *donja* or why it is called *mahala*. Nevertheless, this street is in many ways specific, and unusual; lively and exciting in its own way; neither straight, nor winding; neither short nor too long, and most of the diverse people living there are strange, tragicomic, and fantastic.

Nobody knows when this strange, utterly typical Herzegovinian settlement began. There is no official document that could tell us about the history of Donja Mahala. Or at least, we haven't heard of it. There are only some indications that Donja Mahala is one of the oldest Mostar settlements, established many years before the Ottomans, even before the Romans ruled this area.

A large unsettled part of this street is called simply Harem (Muslim cemetery). Whoever tries to dig in a harem, for whatever reason, will find that underneath a thin layer of soil human bones have lain for centuries, even though no one has been buried there

---

3   The song by Bora Đorđević, a Serbian singer, songwriter, and poet ("Nemoj da ideš mojom ulicom").

for, perhaps, hundreds of years.

Excavation in small dead-end streets, and not only in harems, will discover skulls, clavicles, and all the bones of the thorax. As a result, one could get the impression that the entire street—old, long, and wide as it is—was built on some ancient and unknown cemetery. Not a single soul knows, speaks, or speculates about the people buried there—who they were or when they lived.

They are just speechless, mysterious skeletons under each step we take. They could be anything but they are not few in number.

A Mostar street named after a World War II antifascist, Gojko Vuković, has a modern look. It is inspiring, endemic, and lively in every way, and it is a convenient site for analysis. According to municipal maps, Gojka Vukovića Street starts at the end of Šemovac and at the beginning of Podhum, the part of Mostar between the Franciscan Catholic church and the Old Bridge. However, according to the unmarked but "natural" border, which disregards all official arrangements and lives in the minds of its residents, Donja Mahala starts at Lučki Bridge at Ograda and ends at the Hasana Brkića Bridge in the Čekrk settlement. Mahala stretches on some two thousand meters through the southern part of town, on the right riverbank and at the bottom of steep Hum hill.

Hum rises above the city as some giant hand of stone. A bit of humus and short bush spring from the soil with threatening energies on and around it. There are some fantastic theories according to which Hum is full of flammable sulfur. According to one scenario, which is quite hard to imagine, the Neretva River will either disappear or lose a considerable amount of its water. The sulfur under Hum will ignite, turning the hill into the first Balkan volcano in recent geological history.

This volcano has not yet started shaking the land, and no magma is coming up from inside. But up there on its surface, the destinies of Donja Mahala's various characters are being burnt up and burnt down for undetermined reasons.

It is nice!

Is it?

Why wouldn't it be?

I don't know—maybe because not much is known about my work. It is high time people hear what I had to say. I would like to say something else, as well ... in fact, there is so much I would like to tell you about, but this is an entirely new experience for me. I have no idea how and when to put myself in my world. I surely enjoy this correspondence, but I am not clear who I am corresponding with, with me myself or some separated part of myself. Is this all some kind of schizophrenia or I am possibly talking with ... the localized aspect of God inside me ...

I will repeat it for you, and I will repeat it over and over again: You are talking to your God. Truth is being awakened in you. You are receiving a special inspiration that should break the stereotypes you have lived with for many lives. You have been around for quite some time, and now when I have an opportunity to raise you up, to bring you to myself, I will not miss it. I am possessive, as you know, but endlessly patient, too. You have deliberately left me and in the meantime, influenced by illusion, you have forgotten your eternal relationship with me. Ever since then in every moment, I remembered you and tried to call you back to me. As it is with you, so it is with all other creatures stuck in the material world.

There is one detail here that is not clear to me.

I am listening.

You speak of your eternal desire to take us out of the material world and you also assert that, in my case, I have been rotting for too long in the material world. How can your wish remain unfulfilled? Why don't I come back to you straight away?

We will get back to your question. You talk about my desire. I do not have unfulfilled desires. In my realm, the verb phrase *to desire* is replaced with *to be* or *to have*.

So why isn't it as it should be? What have we been doing while on this planet? And how can you love me without having any expectations from me at the same time? Without expecting something good, nice, and perfect?

And how, in your opinion, would that be?

I believe that we should spend our lives in happiness, good health, and constant fulfillment, in harmony with ourselves and all other beings in touch with us. Shouldn't it be like that?

That's how it should be.

So, why isn't it? I seem to ask more questions than you answer.

Take it easy. I am just listening patiently. I am waiting for you to define your dilemmas. And please don't forget that you are not writing this book for yourself only, and what I have just said mostly refers to your wrong thinking on insufficiently recognized writing. We'll definitely get back to this topic later on.

Now, I will try to clarify some unknowns. First: I don't have unfulfilled desires. All I want, I realize straight away, so I understand the verb *to be* much better than *to desire*. To desire implies enduring, and *wait, suffering,* or *being stuck.*

True love does not contain any kind of unfulfilled desire. It is rather that love contains complete freedom. In the case of love between two people it means mutual freedom. To want someone means to depend on someone, and dependence is yet another undesirable condition. Love is self-sufficiency. Only self-sufficient people are capable of giving themselves to each other completely and endlessly in love. On your way home, that is on your way to me, the first thing you release will be dependence on me. Neither you nor any other adult needs someone else to be complete. The moment you find independence of me will be the moment you understand absolute self-sufficiency.

From that point you will choose your own path, and then you will want only to come to me. And it will be the beginning of your life in happiness, good health, and continual fulfillment, all in accordance with your own self and all other beings.

But I still do not understand why things haven't been like that already, just now, this moment, for me and for all others, as well.

Things are such, and they are not.

Ugh! Do you really want me to say that I see that things truly are not? And personally, I don't see anything that confirms how independence of you leads to you. I am speaking on my own behalf, but I could swear that most people would ask the same question.

Then, I will give you my answer with pleasure.

I am impatient. If you are the One who you say you are, you know my mental state very well. You know that my nerves are shattered.

It could have been worse ... Ha, ha, ha.

What!? Instead of helping, you are doing nothing to help. To laugh at the misery of your own little creatures is not an act God can be proud of.

For the time being, I will say only this: Laugh at your own torment. Laughter relaxes. Truth rustles in laughter. Laughter cures.

And to comment on my earlier statement that a perfect life is true and not true. True, since there has never been a time when you were not complete and perfect by your nature. And not true. Because of an illusion, you have forgotten your original state of happiness and perfection. That is yet another contradiction. And remember, one of the most significant statements so far is: THE TRUTH IS IN CONTRADICTION.

May I make a joke now?

Of course you may, but let me clarify one more thing before you do.

Please do.

For you, I am not the One who I say I am.

Sure, I have known it all the time. I'd better stop this circus. It has anyway gone too far ...

I am stopping you here to repeat: I am the One Femme whom I say I am. You have forgotten that the main idea of this conversation and your book is that I can be a Perfect Wife for you, because I am the Perfect Woman.

Oh! As in "Perfect Woman," the song performed by the Sarajevan band Skroz. Well, at least you have got me back on track.

Yes, I have, but remember I don't want to fly away from you.[4]

You won't, because you would have done it a long time ago, not by plane, but in a spaceship so powerful that only God can use it.
How come I have been in your heart all the time?
Why am I not aware of it?

You were aware of it, but you have forgotten about it. We are just working on it to make you remember again, to achieve self-awareness, and to realize your self-sufficiency. When you return to me, I will prepare a big celebration for you. We will open ourselves to our innermost feelings. I long for you, but I do not want you to do anything that would be against your free will. Remember, I can tell which verbs denote suffering; otherwise, they would not exist. There is nothing existing in its original form that I personally have not created. Everything coming after that is nothing but a free variation of the same theme. The entire universe and all creatures in it are nothing but variations of my ideas.

And again, you are all endlessly free, just as I am free as Goddess. Isn't that perfect? Isn't it the heart of beauty and the magnificence of truth?
I have to admit, I'm speechless!

Really? I thought you were going to make a joke. I'd really love to hear it.

I don't see how a Bosnian joke can fit the magnificence of what you just said.

Before we go on, please change the way you address me. Talk to me as to a female. That will make things easier for both of us. Believe me.

Sure. I prefer talking to a female God rather more than to a male God.

But, it does not mean I am not the male God, too ...

---

4   In the song, a wife flies away from her husband.

… it doesn't mean that you are not the neuter gender God, either. In other words, you are the incomprehensible That One.

That's correct. That's it. You've got it. Each of you has a special relation with me. For some I am him and again, for others, I am That One. Those who try to claim I am not also her are wrong. For you, I am her. So let it be.

I agree. I can't help agreeing with you.

Tell me a joke, then, my dear. You have promised to tell me a joke.

So be it. The joke. Nevertheless, I feel awkward whenever a philosophical discussion—or even part of it—ends with a joke.

You have forgotten what I said in the beginning: AMONG OTHER THINGS, TRUTH IS FOUND IN APPARENTLY TRIVIAL STUFF. That's why I write in capital letters, virtually shouting. You will remember it better this way. Anyway, if truth is in everyday banality, then the everyday is not as banal as we think it is. Banality leads to a sense of purpose.
Tell me that joke, then. I know many are eager to hear it.

A Mujo has had headaches recently and goes to see a doctor. The doctor suggests a brain scan. After the scan, the doctor, feeling a bit uncomfortable, says, "Sir, I don't know how to tell you this, but there is nothing inside your skull, a vacuum, an empty space!" "Well, yes!" Mujo says. "It's better when nothing hurts than when something hurts!"

The same notion can be used in your case: "Better nothing than something!" Truth is in contradictions, but also in an exit from Mind, in one absolute mental Nothing. We can talk about that as well if you would like it. This is just the beginning of the joke.

But, people don't like long jokes.

Who says it's going to be long. Good things never last.

So does that mean that there is no endless beauty?

When one beauty ceases to exist, another might reveal itself. And that is one difference between the material world and a spiritual nature. Enjoyment and beauty are endless and always rising in transcendence.

And to realize that difference between the material world and a spiritual nature, I'd better have my mind free of my thoughts than to be burdened by them.

Yes, you have to get out of your mind, you have to take leave of it. That technique liberates you from suffering, removes worry, and brings mental healing. The more you step away from your mind, the greater chance of coming closer to me. If you want, we can talk about that, too.

Mujo is not that stupid in the end. His conclusion is enlightening. The doctor's reaction remains to be answered.

I am speechless again.

You told me your joke, if nothing else.

Stars and Shit, Victims and Predators

Yesterday you announced that you would say something about mind-controlling techniques. Is it meditation or a way of praying, and is there a risk, in some cases, of the phenomenon called "brainwashing?"

First of all, you should know that your brain is a very powerful tool. All human activities come from the brain. Your brain, at its best, should help you correctly perceive whatever is happening around you. What's more powerful is intelligence and above intelligence comes a spiritual particle, which is the center of all energies and the basis of the basis of what you are.

When functioning correctly, the primary stimuli to think, choose, and act come from the highest level; that is, from the soul. However, beneath your mind, but at the highest level of cellular function, are your five senses: sight, hearing, smell, taste, and touch. And for the long while that illusory material was fascinating you and distracting you. Your spirit had little influence on your decisions.

In the meantime, the stimuli to which you attached great importance registered only at the basest level, ending at your cells and senses. You lost touch with your higher nature.

Spiritual amnesia set in as you have turned away from me. Even though many spiritual advisors call that process *"banishment from paradise"* or a divine curse, it was only and always your own deliberate decision to renounce me. Yet those spirits that don't turn away, that always reside in the spiritual realm, are not closer to me. Nor do I like them more than I like you. My love fulminates unconditionally in all directions. It is the basis of existence for all material and spiritual worlds, as well as the countless souls that dwell in them. The material world is not a jail for *disobedient souls,* as many *spiritual leaders* declare. In neither the material nor spiritual world is there a hell, although I am credited with having created such places for additional punishment.

How could I be an all-merciful God if I created agonizing infernal worlds where I imprisoned souls that *misuse* the freedom of choice I granted them? In such a case, there would be neither your free will nor my all-encompassing mercy. Everything would be a farce. And I am not the God of farce.

You have got off the track a bit while answering my question, if I may say so. Nevertheless, what you're saying is really interesting, especially because I have always thought of myself as a renegade and sinner, recipient of numerous divine punishments.

Yes, the number of setbacks is anything but small, even though I am tackling only topics related to mental issues. They are the basis of all the problems in the world where you live.

I absolutely agree. What God of love would you be if you would not direct us, gives us kind advice and guidance, right?

That's exactly what I am doing with each of you, and your number is endless. My patience, gentleness, mildness (as you call it), good nature, love, and mercy are endless, and I have showered them on you. Not only on you throughout eternity, but on all other living creatures in endless worlds. Now I would like to continue with my previous explanations.

Oh, yes! Of course! I apologize for the interruption.

There is nothing you could do that you would have to ask my forgiveness for. There is nothing I can do, and still owe one my apology. You are not capable of doing anything wrong to anyone that you would have to apologize for. Nobody has ever done anything to you that he has to ask forgiveness for.

I don't understand much of what you just said, except for perhaps your second claim.

If you don't understand it, it means that the energy of your acting, thinking, and existing does not come from the center of what you are, from infallible spirit. On the contrary, you perceive the world around you through unstable senses and wrong mental distinctions. Your perception is wrong, but it can still be corrected. In fact, that process is not necessarily wrong or useless.

To act from the position of the senses means to submit to spiritual oblivion, and spiritual oblivion is necessary for a complete perception of self, me, and my world that is surrounding us. How to understand Absolute Truth if you have never been in the great lie atmosphere; how can you know what happiness is if you had not seemingly suffered in misery; how can you climb up if there is not a point determining a lower level?

Therefore, you, the temporary residents in illusion, I like you, adventurers, very much because it is not only about that that you understand your own real nature of eternally happy, blissed and powerful people through your own self but through misery, powerlessness, and a nonexisting blissfulness you are experiencing.

I, your God, realize my own endless possibilities through my creatures' experiences. There is nothing that you have experienced in your bodily adventure, temporary as it is, that I have escaped. It is my experience too because I am deep in your heart. We are in a symbiotic project that each of you creatures will finish. This is my promise. Nobody will be condemned to suffer in an eternal hell. Nobody will be banished from God's kingdom. Make it known to your friends and to your enemies, too.

As enmity is only a distorted perception of one segment of love without which we would never be able to understand the

true nature of friendship or complete openness of love.

A great explanation. Fantastic description of cosmology. Short, clear, and simple.

My wisdom is not only mine, it's yours, too—inherent in all. Do not redirect your energy from your deceptive senses to your mind (so prone to error) and then get stuck there where you will be lost in your intellect with no connection whatsoever to your soul.

How can I turn that course around? How can I make sure that the energy comes out from its natural source, my soul?

Do you see how we nicely got back to your initial question related to this issue?

Yes, I do! And that fascinates me even more. I simply can't figure out where all these overwhelming thoughts and profound philosophy come from each time I sit at my computer. I have always thought that God addressed only the chosen ones, only the exalted prophets, purified gurus, in their temples, mosques, or churches or blessed places—the Hill of Sinay, Mekka, or Vrindavan.

Here is how I was taught: Be humble, because you are nobody and nothing. Only a guru's or God's unconditional mercy can get you out of the cesspool that is material existence. You are guilty and sinful and full to the top with your dirty thoughts and actions. Your bad karma is insurmountable. Only with the humility of a worm may you acquire your teacher's mercy because God will not even look at you without the mediation of his immaculate representative.

But they never managed to agree about which teachers were right, which clergy were enlightened, which gurus were authorized to save souls. No global, inter-religious congress has decided which way is correct. Every religious group or sect is convinced that it is the right one, Christian, Hindu, Jew, or Muslim. All others go to hell or, in the best case, go on waiting to reincarnate into other, more or less intelligent bodies. I sense that nobody is wrong. It could be true, at least, that only one side is correct, that everyone is on his path of cognition and that everyone is guaranteed paradise sooner or later. If I understood you, that's your promise, isn't it?

No.

Now you say, "No." How come?

Simple. My promise doesn't offer paradise. My promise is of an inevitable return to me, but I am not in paradise.

I don't understand. Isn't paradise promised to all because that is where you are found? If you are not in paradise, then where are you?

In a localized sense I am in the heart of all living creatures and in every atom of spiritual or material world. There is me in everything, and there is nothing in me. As you may detect, this is yet another mystical contradiction. My nonpersonal essence showers everything that I have created—endless suns, galaxies, and stars. I am the impersonal glow of Brahmajyoti.[5] In my infinite number of personal transcendental forms I revel in spiritual energies of mystical worlds, Vaikuntha,[6] which stretch through endless space and inexpressible time. There is my home, and there is your departure point. Paradisiac planetary systems lie in magnificent and grandiose galactic spaces between central planetary systems of your material world and the impersonal Brahmajyoti adjacent to a transcendental empire. Thus, the promise I made doesn't offer paradisiac systems, but hold open a God's world that is above all. For you, this is the easiest way to explain the division of space. Here it is in your language, with its limited expression.

Hmm ... I am trying to create a sort of graph to represent that I have just heard.

My suggestion is that you do not try to draw graphs. Anything that could be represented by a chart would be too far from

---

5   Brahmajyoti, spiritual glow coming from the transcendental body of God, impersonal aspect of God, Sanskrit.

6   Vaikuntha, eternal planets in spiritual worlds, Sanskrit.

the truth. There is no point risking wrong interpretations. How can you draw Vaikuntha worlds that are less than an inch away from you? I am in your heart through my localized world, and the blessed trackless spiritual worlds are there, too, because my residence is in them, as well. Space and time are relative the way you see them. Everything takes place now and everything is in one point of all-permeating space expanding in all directions to infinity. Nothing happens that is not taking place now. There is nothing at one place that it is not at any place at the same time. Your graphs cannot help. They are less than useless.

All space and time are in one, the only one center of your being—and I am there, too. And when I speak about Paradise or Hell, I refer more to the state of your consciousness than to a particular space. Paradise, Hell, and Vaikuntha[7]—all of them reflect the state of your consciousness as well as of the level of creation of your mind. Therefore, it is important to gain a transcendent mind.

When I say "get out of one's mind," I don't mean to neglect or destroy your mind. I refer to raising mental awareness, mind enlightenment. Therefore, some meditation techniques are vital and always available.

Now we can talk about controlling one's own mind. Your happiness or suffering is proportionately equal to the effectiveness of that control. When life stimuli start again from spirit, over intelligence, toward mind and senses, you become aware of me and of course, by that, of yourself, because we are One, even though we are different.

I have the impression that reorienting energy between spirit and senses leads to mind control. Is that the point?

Exactly.

That is a task to be undertaken in your mind. It will not be easy. Through eons and your many lives, your mind was dysfunctional. It thought on only the material, the physical plane, which caused its dysfunction and by that, its mental dysfunction. You forgot the incomprehensibly greater beauty and power of spiritual joy. You acted in complete *spiritual*

---

7   Sanskrit—endless spiritual universe.

amnesia. You lost me. You have lost yourself. But, do not condemn what went on in inside you. As I have already indicated, what you need is oblivion if you want to fully comprehend the blessing of memory. You have to forget me, in order to fully comprehend in a repeated comprehension my significance for your existence. You are not cursed, forgotten, rejected, punished, locked up; you have never been such nor could it ever happen. You are not forgotten. Your state of forgetfulness is temporary, but various meditations can save you from oblivion and reactivate spiritual energy.

Many find it a difficult task; many back away. Even persistent people do not enjoy quick fruits of their efforts. But all complete their important work sooner or later. It is your only destiny, your only unchangeable destiny because you yourself have chosen it that way.

Which ways of meditation or prayer are best? Are there any religions or spiritual movements whose teachings and techniques are more advanced than others?

If I were to put any religion or culture before or after another in some imaginary spiritual hierarchy, everything I said earlier would make no sense. Some do set their religion on an imaginary pedestal of bogus spiritual value. And they are not first followers of the religious community they belong to. Clerics who support any kind of religious discrimination will not be able to identify themselves with any sentence in this book that we are jointly creating at this blessed moment.

At the same time, each of the more or less *official religions* on this planet has preserved wisdom, in its scripture, that can lead to sincere prayer. Some learned men such as Dr. Murphy used to call it scientific prayer. And I agree with it. You might find good, defined methods of using meditation and prayer in books such as *The Power of Positive Thinking.*[8]

And you will not be talking about it here anymore.

Of course I will. First of all, it is an extremely valuable psychological practice. Inspired meditation is the key to spiritual fulfillment and material prosperity. The irony is

---

8   By Norman Vincent Peale.

that material prosperity becomes insignificant when spiritual fulfillment is revitalized.

The more we rise spiritually, the more we give up material values?

Giving up is a tough way of suppressing desire. As a rule, giving up turns into violence against your own self. I suggest you never give up anything except, perhaps, the practice of giving up.
When I speak about the nonexistence of material desires, I speak about nonexistence. It is impossible to be in a completely desire-free state. Spiritual revival refers to desiring the transformation process. Transform from one level to another, from material to transcendental, from the outside world to the inside one, and your happiness will be in you and not outside. Many have already experienced it, and they know what I am talking about.
Giving up is an act of violence against mind. But transforming desire elevates mentality. When you do, you will not have the urge to renounce or give up anything. Material enjoyment will no longer be something you strive for. The stimuli for your energy will no longer spring from five reckless senses, but from a single blessed spirit.
Oblivion has relinquished the place to memory and once you transcend material universes and raise to spiritual space, you will never again get back under the influence of illusion because you have become aware of the oppositeness to perfection—one big *relative*—only then is perfection being revealed in its full sense. You have returned to your own God forms. You are Gods.

So far I heard the theory that we embrace the material world because we want to renounce you as our God, that we want to be small gods in the material world, that we rebel against you out of envy and resentment because of your sacrosanct, supreme position and authority.

Now, I will ask you a few questions and you answer them. Will you?

Why not, if I know the answers.

Don't complicate your life with how you will respond. Just follow your inner intuition and sound logic. These two in combination always yield a satisfying result.

I'll try to follow your advice.

Do you agree with the theory that your envy of God and desiring to become a god yourself pushed you away from me? Were you banished?

As far as I know, most established religions agree about that although each teaches its own myth about it.

It is interesting that all your religions agree upon those claims that are absolutely untrue.

Does this mean we are not banished from paradise? The myth about Adam and Eve and Adam and Hawa is untrue?

Take it easy. Now it still is my turn to ask questions and yours to answer.

Oh, yes. Please forgive me!

I have nothing to forgive you, especially your noticeable curiosity. But listen, is the explanation logical? You are in absolute perfection, but all of a sudden you become envious of my position as your Supreme God?

When you give it more thought, there should be no place for such a low emotion such as envy in the state of Absolute Perfection.

Exactly. So, assuming that my home is a perfect home, it is not possible for there to exist envy or any other negative quality that poisons the blissfulness of love. Therefore, let's move on. If envy or any negative emotion is impossible, what could have happened to make you forget me, lose your true self, or reduce your residence from an absolute to a relative level? In other words, if the reasons for your *fall* into *the world of darkness* do not include envying me or disobeying me, what could have caused it at all?

I can't answer that question. I am afraid I don't get it.

All right. I'll give you a light push. The absolute excludes the relative. Do you agree?

Yes.

Perfection excludes imperfection. Do you agree with this, as well?

Of course.

The state of complete internal happiness means that there is no place for misery at all.

Right. I agree.

True love leaves no space for envy, jealousy, narrow-mindedness, or hatred.

That's how it should be.

It's not that things should be that way. They have always been that way.

Then, I can't but agree with you—with whatever you are saying.

With me, you always have the possibility to choose, dear.

Well, then, I choose to agree with you.

That's good. What could have happened to you to make you go away from me, even temporarily, but still go away from me? You exist and enjoy a perfect place with a perfect person under perfect conditions. Nevertheless, for some reason, you have decided that the best thing would be to change your existence, even though there was nothing between the two of us except pure and inexhaustible love that we enjoyed endlessly.

I have to admit: I *can't follow* you. I *will help* you understand because you want me to. Well, you have graceful me, true love, and completeness of perfection. What could have made us move you to the position opposite from perfection, where you will lose it all, be it even temporarily?

Just a moment … Perhaps it's the fact that we will never be able to experience perfection unless we understand imperfection.

Correct! Correct! That's it. We are on the way to guessing the meaning and dynamics of how things stand now, how they were, and how they will be, and the definition is universal: IF YOU EXPERIENCE ONE EXTREME, YOU WILL INEVITABLY UNDERSTAND ITS OPPOSITE. What took you down is not the envy or hatred toward me but the deepest and the sincerest urge to fully understand how big and fantastic is the love that you feel for me. Through your experiencing of lower energies, I, as well, learn more about myself, since I am still in you, sharing with you all your experiences, regardless of the fact that you have temporarily forgotten me.

You have moved away from my love and then you have embraced me even more tightly.

And when we are not together, we are still together, and then we are together again more than we have ever been.

Love set us apart and it will bring us together again. Or more precisely, the search for a complete love will.

And that's why I love you, dear. I really love you and yearn after you.

I long to see you return …

And I will have to be honest with you, completely honest, first of all for myself, but also for all the other people who might read this sometime, and of course for you most of all.

Sincerity is the greatest virtue.

After all my life as I remember it, after many tragedies I have suffered, my emotions have become almost completely numb. Dear Goddess, I would like you to have a name, I have lost feeling for many natural states, not only for elevated thoughts about which we keep discussing. I have stopped feeling things at all and, instead of growing, my perceptions have become more and more limited. Now, I wouldn't like anyone to get the wrong idea. Long before I started writing this book, I had been suffering a lot due to poor circumstances and, most of all, my own perpetual weakness. It is not important now how bad things happened to me. What's important is that I did not have a positive response to many of life's temptations. As a result my nerves shattered and I was in a terrible condition.

If your heart stops beating, you leave your body. If you stop breathing, you die. If you get cancer, you die slowly. It is certain that death is waiting around the corner, and it is only a matter of time before it comes to you. In many cases death comes as a sort of liberation, a release, an end to suffering—almost a resolution. But when your nerves start cracking, as a rule you start losing control and can have a nervous breakdown. When this happens, you can't be sure that you will surmount your suffering through death. As a chronic mental patient you might live a long—very long—miserable life deprived of all or most human emotions. To be incapable of perceiving life while living, that is hell. Those are the moments when I feel absolutely far from you, when I even doubt that you will ever help me. I imagine you as uninterested in helping me, since you are perfect, and you have your perfect chosen ones—prophets, gurus, masters, teachers—and I am not one of them.

I am just an ordinary guy. I have to live my destiny, whether I like it or not. I am powerless before my destiny. There is no way I can get rid of bad karma except through inexpressible suffering. Who knows what bad things I did in my past lives, so that I have to deal with horrible consequences? One way or another, emotions are gone, and I envy you for your continued living in the perfect world. I have become envious, my darling. It is not impossible as I am back in the relative world now. I have the right to envy; it is not illogical here.

And why do I envy you? Because you can feel, you yearn, you kiss … All your endless emotions are still with you. And what about me? I can't tell you that I love you, because all I feel now is depression and fear. I have a problem with psychomotor skills. I am taking pills. It's not that I am not grateful for this unusual writing adventure. I don't have to convince you of that. But I am bitter because at the moment I can't feel the great joy of meeting you again in this way. And I am obviously the coauthor of an extraordinary and wonderful letter. Even though I am sure you are encouraging me to make something good and positive for myself, I still feel that my feelings are not appropriate to the role given to me. When will I start feeling as I should? I would be so happy if I could tell you, "I love you!" But all I feel is difficulty talking and numbness in the top of my head. My hands are shaking. *What* is going on? What is *going on*? Explain it to me, please. Now, more than ever, I need your explanation, your healing words.

I do understand you, I fully understand you, but before I say anything else, I will need your consent for only one thing.

I am ready.

Your consent that you will never and for no reason feel less valuable than others, if you need my assistance, love, or support.

I will try.

It is not only an arbitrary thought, but a whole truth.

Thank you. I think this will make me feel better.

We will be talking now about illness, whether mental or physical, and its underlying cause.

The fact that I am suffering mentally does not mean I am less worthy to be addressed by you?

Can we please go back to a previously mentioned truth? When you need my assistance, love, or support, never and for no reason should you feel less worthy than others to use my blessing.

I knew it would not go smoothly in my case.

I think I should also point out that this truth is universal. It applies to all living creatures including human beings.

That's the way it is, I suppose.

Now you can be sure.

One more question.

As many as you wish. Each question is a guideline for truth if

you sincerely pursue it.

As I suffer emotionally from time to time—sometimes more, sometimes less—is it unusual that I have not obtained healing in the moment that I start talking to you?

If something is happening in your life, the way it happens, when it happens, and how long it lasts, please remember that the event itself is a perfect condition that will take you to a complete sense of that event. This means that you should not feel bad because you did not touch stars the very moment you started writing this document. There is a perfect time for everything. Every event, as I pointed out, makes sense for itself. You are expected only to recognize and accept the significance. I repeat that there is a time for everything under the sun. Everything fits in perfectly, even if you do not discern perfection. When it happens, remember that the perfect time has come for you to experience suffering temporarily due to the illusion of detachment. Even when you think you are lost forever and there is no way out, in such dark times keep it in mind that your suffering is only temporary. This especially applies to various weaknesses and illnesses you live with sometimes. From the point of view of relativity, that time sometimes lasts too long, and so does the long-term suffering of chronic disease.

Deep in yourself, you chose it yourself hoping to achieve the Absolute or complete and final reshaping of your suffering. In other words, the point of suffering is to understand what life is without suffering. It surely does not mean that we should disregard suffering and negativities as it is simply impossible to do it. The nature of pain is such that it constantly points to its own painful action. As soon as any kind of suffering appears in your experience, your spirit immediately starts working toward freeing itself from it, even though your spirit brought it there temporarily. In the nature of the spirit, there is no place for suffering; the spirit is an eternal enjoyer. You will free yourself of misery once you understand the causes of that suffering. It is not always immediately obvious, so you experience a period of suffering.

Can we deliberately reduce how long suffering lasts?

Yes, if we discern and timely influence the causes of suffering.

But, you said the cause is not always obvious right away.

What takes place then is the time of suffering, and I would add—limited time of suffering.

But how can one effectively limit the limited time of suffering?

By discerning the causes of suffering and acting accordingly.

I think your answers go around in circles.

Your questions are going around in circles, and I am just answering them. The same applies to suffering and with all your persistent and hopeless attempts to run away from me, to disregard yourself, and healing truth even though it tries to get your attention.

I am trying and want to use it, but obviously, I am not being successful in that attempt. Encourage me.

Of course, my dear. Go a few questions back and see where you asked the same questions.

Yes! You are fantastic. I was too blind to see it. You don't repeat answers. I am the one going round in circles with the same questions.

But not even that is a problem because questions always lead to truth. Each time you go back to the same question, you will be directed to the same path until you get it. My patience is gentle and eternal—use it.

I will try. Well, how can you recognize the signs of suffering and react to them in a timely way? What does it mean to react in a timely way? Does it mean you can also be late when reacting to causes of suffering? And if you are, what are the possible consequences?

New questions—new answers. The viciousness of one circle has disappeared. I am not saying that there will be no more vicious circles but use me each time you feel you reach a dead-end. That's what I am here for. Always, Now, and Forever.

Even when I appear not to be here by your side and not to be taking care of you, or when I seem to be too far away or do not exist at all, especially at dark times, reach into the deepest part of yourself and calm your restless mind. That very mind, in its confusion and fear, is posing obstacles and creating illusions. Calm it down. Convince it of the veracity of the contradictions to every possible fear haunting it. Do it long enough; do it gently and patiently (with no expectations whatsoever) and it will eventually start attending to your words of tranquility, logic, and truth and go back to normal. Getting back to a normal state of mind will get you first to yourself, and then to me. We will break another bottle, reach an agreement, and break out another vicious circle, one at a time, once and forever.

Oh! Wonderful! Really wonderful! Help me achieve it then. Please. Don't leave me. Don't leave me ever. Make me always feel somehow that you are here, by my side, that you don't leave me, that you understand my every problem and suffering, regardless of what they are, and that you will protect and heal me.

Be comforted that it is always so. It has always been so, except you were not comforted when you suffered the illusion of detachment. You read about it in Walsch's *Communion with God*. The illusion of detachment is one of the most devastating illusions unless you recognize it as it really is—an illusion. The illusion of detachment, if taken as real, causes all your suffering, illnesses, all your worry, setbacks, weakness, and mental anxiety. The illusion of detachment is the bunker of guilt and fear. Guilt and fear, as you have read, are your only enemies.

The illusion of detachment. I remember that. I had Walsch's book in my hands a year ago, or more, but I didn't understand at the time the true meaning of the illusion of detachment. Can illusion be the notion mentioned in the ancient Vedic texts as maya?

The maya, simulacrum, illusion are variations on the same idea. Illusion refers to something that doesn't exist, of course. It deludes the observer. The maya confuses one with an impression of reality that is utterly false, that has nothing

51

to do with reality. And that distortion frightens a confused mind. When that sets in, one responds to misconceptions of reality with wrong choices.

The mind strays from the truth and merges with illusion until the body's natural reactions completely disappear. A *breakdown* results. By manipulating a weakened mind, the maya causes fear; fear creates guilt (or one of the other negative emotions). When fear and guilt are treated inappropriately, all kinds of physical and mental diseases result. A weakened mind is unstable and susceptible to confusion. It becomes chronically dissatisfied, fearful, and disturbed. A weakened mind is a hotbed of problems.

Such a mind will create conditions in which an elephant will shrink from a mouse; ears will never hear silence; eyes will not see the photons in a beam of light. Such a mind causes dizziness, insecurity, anxiety, depression, mania, phobias, and hallucinations. Let it happen to you, and you will be afraid of the dark, horror movies, ghosts, hospitals, injections, and strangers. You will lose self-confidence and be sick all the time, will consult false healers and cunning doctors. The pharmaceutical industry will profit by you; the military industry will thrive on your war madness; vice will flourish.

Truth about each creature's cause of suffering is hidden where it can be found. And the sooner you get to the real cause of personal suffering, the sooner you will banish it. There is no time limit for finding it. If you delay looking for it, you just miss chances to shorten your suffering. In my world eventual freedom is guaranteed; my love for all a sure thing.

I think things are clearing up for me now. Your words are reaching my heart and mind. This is the first time I have seen my mind/ intellect as the weakest part of my being. It has been difficult to define *mind*, but now it seems to exist separately, even though it is still an essential part of me. And what is most important: I discern how my own fantasies and delusions have brought me chronic mental pain. Disease begins in the mind. A negative mind feeds all kinds of weakness. Therefore, my crucial questions now are: How does one control one's mind and move it from darkness to light? Is there some kind of mental exercise for that? In the *Bhagavad-Gita*, Krishna said something like this: "Mind is either your best friend or your most dangerous enemy." I think I understand that idea much better now. How can I make my mind my humble friend, instead of my bitter enemy? Isn't it the key question? Please give me the best answer.

No and no. Those are the answers to your last two questions. No one question is more important than another. The same applies to responses. The first step of a staircase is no less important than the one in the middle or perhaps the one at the top. You ask practical questions to hear useful responses, but there is no such thing as a "key question" or a "best answer." Likewise, there is no "greatest among men," no animal is more or less valuable than the others, and plants are not more valuable than insects. Not a single molecule in creation is more or less valuable than any other. And that is truth. Accept this if you want to calm your mind. God's world is the world of no segregation at all. Haven't you noticed that your mind is most happily at rest when you are relieving yourself? Organs and their functions are all connected.

Now there's something I *don't* want to talk about with God, especially not with Madam Goddess! It is not appropriate for everyday talk, let alone conversation with the Almighty! I don't want to get into that kind of freaky communication!

Well, then, we'll come to that in due course. And, to you I am not a matron lady or spinster. I am a young lady no matter what we talk about. Even when we seem to be separated, the part of my personality that is destined for you waits and yearns for you. Can you accept that I created your body and every other human body, too?

I can't imagine anything different than that.

Good. Is your colon part of my creation, as well?

That would seem logical.

And it is. The truth is logical. I will keep asking you questions. Do you accept my being as an active element in every single atom of the entire and infinite creation?

Whatever refers to God is all-permeating.

You understand it so well. Is your waste part of the entire infinite creation?

I am avoiding the answer in order to avoid your next question. I see what you are up to. This is too uncomfortable for me. I am afraid of a big, unforgivable sin.

Then I will do it for you, in order for you to avoid fictitious responsibility. The truth is, my dear, that I am the Creator and elementary part of each execrated atom ...

Hold it, hold it, hold it! This is too much for me! This is very disturbing for me, very disturbing indeed. Can we skip this topic? Why can't we talk about planets, stars, galaxies, black holes, pulsars, super nova, galactic fog, and everything else that is so magnificent, beautiful, and a part of your fantastic creation?

You are segregating my creation. You belittle and deny me when you judge one part of my creation to be less valuable than another. No wonder, then, that you think that there are more or less valuable questions. Segregation continues so whites are valued differently than blacks; men are more valuable than women; gold is more valuable than salt; and water is more valuable than fire. Jennifer Lopez, wealthy in the spotlight, is more important than a Sudanese mother dying of hunger. Don't some in your country think Christians are better than Muslims? Don't others value them vice versa?

In relation to Absolute Truth, nothing that is better or worse, up or down, right or left. From the same elementary substances I have made shiny stars spread around the dark night sky and a malodorous piece of excrement.

I am losing consciousness ...

Once you recover, I will say it again for you: FROM THE SAME ELEMENTARY SUBSTANCES I HAVE MADE SHINING STARS SPREAD AROUND THE DARK NIGHT SKY AND THE MALODOROUS PIECE OF EXCREMENT THAT YOU EXCRETE.

There are more truths: SEGREGATION IS YET ANOTHER CAUSE OF YOUR SUFFERING.

NOT A SINGLE ITEM OF THE ENTIRE CREATION IS

MORE OR LESS VALUABLE THAN ANY OTHER ITEM IN SPACE OR TIME.

THERE IS NOTHING SUCH AS GOOD OR BAD, UP OR DOWN, RIGHT OR LEFT IN RELATION TO THE ABSOLUTE TRUTH.

If you think I am *not* an active part of an atom in every existing particle, then you accept the lie that something can be separate from me. You may also wrongly suppose that there is a certain lower-level creator in relation to me or even opposed to me. You may accept the existence of a devil or shaitan.[9]

My truth is THERE IS NOTHING SEPARATE FROM ME. I AM THE ONLY CREATOR. THE DEVIL IS A FABRICATION.

I don't know what to say. Everything you are talking about is so logical.

THE TRUTH IS IN LOGIC. WHENEVER YOU DISREGARD LOGIC, YOU WILL APPEAL TO PAIN, YOU WILL APPEAL TO SUFFERING. WHENEVER YOU DISREGARD LOGIC, YOU WILL DISREGARD ME.

I am speechless again. I am admiring you. I admire …

Admire yourself, because you are my creation. I admire you, too, because you are my own creation. Qualitatively, you are equal to me. You are a divine creature. Even while you are sitting on a toilet and relieving yourself, while you are brushing your teeth, eating chocolate, or drinking blueberry juice, while you are walking, sitting, or running (you should practice the latter one more often or you should walk more). While you are making love with your girlfriend, while you are playing with your child, while you are laughing or crying, each moment of your life is blessed. All is part of one perfect process. When your life doesn't seem to make sense and it looks miserable, appeal to God's logic, appeal to my name, and I will make sure things get easier for you and you will find the way.

Is that your promise? Is that your guarantee for all people I know

---

9   In Muslim countries, the devil or an evil spirit.

or I don't know?

There has never been a time when things were not such and they will always be like that as long as we exist. Start hoping I exist, then believe in my being with you and finally, remember that there has never been a time when things were not such. I can't disclose myself to anyone who doesn't want me to be disclosed to him. To all those who think I am a distant and uninterested God, I will remain a question mark until the moment they hear my words which I keep whispering into their ear: "I'm here. By your side. I love you unconditionally. I have always been yearning for you. Listen to my words and join me in fantastic living."

You say these things continuously to everyone?

Just choose to hear me, if there is even the slightest ray of hope, raise it so that I can address you [male/female speaking], and I will do it in such a clear and neat way that you will not be able to deny it. Why wouldn't it be like that? Please tell me at least one reason why it shouldn't it be like that?

I suppose that a person can be quite sinful.

Give me one example.

There are many examples. I think that my country Bosnia and Herzegovina is full of such examples. From 1992 to 1995, the world witnessed the dreadful war which happened here. Even today, I am still unable to understand what could have made so many people commit crimes of such terrible magnitude and bloody their hands to such an extent. You know it very well that during the war in Bosnia and Herzegovina a large number of innocent civilians was killed. At least 100,000 Muslims were killed by Serb and Croat nationalists. The simple truth is that Serbs and Croats were killed, as well. It was no small number of people from each side who died, but the fact is that Bosnian Muslims paid the highest price in the Balkan war. While I am writing this, Radovan Karadžić and Ratko Mladićhave are still the most wanted war criminals today. Many war crimes have already been processed at the International Court in the Hague, Netherlands. The war in Bosnia and Herzegovina, similar to others waged elsewhere in the world at any time, clearly showed how some people at a critical historical period when anarchy grew dramatically, curtailed the freedom and lives of other people for the most trivial and primitive reasons. Succumbing to base instincts, I'd say. Concentration camps were opened, and people were executed on a massive scale. Srebrenica is a malicious wound of contemporary history. Women were raped; babies, pregnant women, young men, and the infirm were killed; houses were burned and bridges destroyed. In May 1993, the Old Bridge of Mostar was destroyed. Some fifteen years ago, terrible things happened here such as genocide, religious fanaticism, Nazism, and urbicide. Do people whose goal in life was to cause death, hatred, and fear in a most brutal manner deserve to be addressed with the following words: "I'm here, by your side. I love you unconditionally. I have always yearned for you. Listen to my words and join me in the fantastic character of living?"

It's not that I am not addressing the so-called criminals, too, but as long as a person acts contrary to the basic rules of living, he will never be able to hear my words. He will feel lost in the deepest illusions. His choices will be useless and completely wrong.

What are the basic rules of living and how come you suddenly use the word "wrong?" Hasn't it been said that nothing and nobody can be right or wrong in relation to the Absolute?

Let's put first things first. Here we speak about a very sensitive topic. I can't afford incorrect interpretations and therefore, I will do my best to be completely clear. Basic rules of living are the following:

1. NEVER DO TO OTHERS WHAT YOU WOULD NOT LIKE THEM TO DO TO YOU.

2. YOUR FREEDOM ENDS WHERE ANOTHER LIVING CREATURE'S BEGINS.

These universal and eternal rules have always been there. There will be no time when they are not applicable. It is impossible to do anything and not to be subject to these rules at the same time. Their source is in the simple and magnificent

truth that I repeated on several occasions: WE ARE ALL ONE. This means that it is impossible to hurt anyone and not to hurt yourself at the same time. On the other hand, each time you curtail the freedom of someone else, you curtail your own freedom. If you hit or hurt another person, it is as if you hurt and hit yourself, as you and he are one, and you will have the reaction through the consequence that will come sooner or later.

There is nothing that would be wrong but we can aspire to incorrect action on a temporary basis. A wrong may imply damage beyond repair; an incorrect is always subject to instantaneous correction, an instantaneous healing. So, when I say *wrong*, take it as something incorrect but possible to fix at all times.

Why don't we feel the consequences immediately? If people felt the pain at the time they hurt other people, they would not dare commit any crime or injury to their fellow men. I think it would be more efficient that way.

If efficiency is the goal, you might ask why I don't appear on this planet in person to give justice directly.

That could work.

I would violate the second basic rule of living by doing that, and the rule applies to me as much as to you, since we are the same when the concept is applied. If consequences occurred reflexively and concurrently, you would lose your freedom to think and do what you want.

I don't want coercion to influence choice in the world. Rather experience must *instruct* choice. Coercion takes freedom away; experience creates wisdom. If a criminal does not stop criminal behavior because he prefers good and natural consequences instead, but rather stops out of fear of immediate punishment, then he will never actually choose not to be a criminal. He will merely have been forced to stop. He would still be a criminal if circumstances permitted.

Coercion doesn't convey insight into life. But a natural consequence offers experience that leads to wisdom. The more we understand, the more we remember.

Does the pendulum of consequence imply that a victim was a predator at some time in the past? Were the victims of the Srebrenica massacre on the other side of the bloody model in their past lives?

One should be particularly careful here. If I say that the victim was once a predator, then some would justify their crimes. It would not be a useful experience. But if I say that victims were innocent of harming others, then the next logical question would be "Why are there any victims at all?" Killing would seem pointless, and killing is almost always pointless. Therefore, I will take a contrarian position. The answer to your question about "victims as previous predators" is both yes or no at the same time. Remember one of the important statements: TRUTH IS IN CONTRADICTION.

It would appear that you are avoiding a concrete answer.

Contradictory truths are the way to avoid only one answer. Don't always take things and events from an either/or position. Such views limit your perspective. Take into consideration two or more possibilities and gain wisdom from each of them. That's how a mosaic is developed and the whole truth can emerge. I'll go back to a concrete example and concede that a hypothetical victim used to be a predator. He understands the real position of a victim through his experience and wishes never to take a predatory role. At the same time, an illusory victim is only illusory. His position as a victim will sooner or later be taken by an illusory predator who will know the suffering victim's position. That experience will teach him that choosing to be a predator is not a good choice. Even though he is not a real victim, he empathizes as one.

Why illusory victim, why illusory predator? It is difficult to talk about illusion to a true victim of a crime. How can one explain to a mother from Srebrenica that her child was only an illusory victim of an illusory criminal? I wouldn't dare to say something like that to the victims.

Neither you nor I nor anyone else can communicate one word if someone doesn't want to hear it. We are, however, able to say what our interlocutor is willing to listen to. Here, we are

not discussing the strictly legal aspect of a crime, but rather its esoteric aspect. But spiritual understanding of a problem includes its legal solution. Therefore, try to understand me. I don't mouth platitudes. My explanations are not partial. I approach all events from one and only one position: the truth.

But not even I have the right to speak truth to anyone, including a mother from Srebrenica, if that person doesn't want to absorb a bigger picture framed by truth. If we disregard illusions, if we exclude maya, then each one in this world is a predator or victim in relation to someone else. A Chetnick against a mother from Srebrenica; a Mujahedin against a Serb civilian in Sarajevo; an Ustasha against a sniper's victim at the Mostar Kamenica Bridge. Unfortunately, there are many such examples, a myriad indeed: Hutu opposed to Tutsi and vice versa. An American against an Afghanistani and vice versa. An Englishman against an Irishman and vice versa. Muslims against Hindus and vice versa. Jews against Muslims and vice versa. Shias against Sunnis. Catholics against Protestants. One may go further than that and say that animals are the prey of the meat industry; drug users are the prey of drug dealers; children are the prey of pedophiles; fish of fishermen; ozone is being destroyed by toxic chemicals. What is particularly alarming is the fact that this list of prey and predators could continue all the way until the end of this conversation and still be incomplete. If illusions blind us, then what remains is only one horrible planet with extremely unhappy people who live there. For those who are blinded by illusion, there will soon be nothing left.

But, my claim is unquestionable; my speech is beyond dispute: ILLUSIONS EXIST, AND THE DEEPER YOU ARE IN THEM, THE LESS YOU ARE AWARE OF THEM, AND THE MORE DISTANT YOU GET FROM YOURSELVES, FROM ME, AND FROM ABSOLUTE TRUTH, IN GENERAL. The two greatest illusions are the illusion of detachment and the illusion of insufficiency. You have read about them in the Walsch book *Communion with God*.

Yes. I remember. Can I have some additional explanations?

Always. We shall apply the illusion of detachment and the

illusion of insufficiency to a concrete example of a mother from Srebrenica whose six-month-old baby was illusorily killed.

I wish the examples were less painful …

I wish you suffered less due to the illusion of pain. Nothing is as it appears at first glance. Whatever happens on the way to finality has a different appearance than it will have in the end.

… even though I can't deny that such a difficult case will be an interesting way to analyze the function and impact of illusion.

Please try not to use words such as "pain, difficulty, evil, weakness, a lack of power, or bad feeling." Or don't use them too often. Uttering a word releases energy that materializes through a reflexive process, because a word is a form of vibrating energy. Negative words magnify negative energy and vice versa. Nothing you do, think, or say is neutral or unproductive. Each word you utter about a particular topic reveals something about you in relation to the subject of discussion; that vibrating energy is a product of your thought; your thought determines your position in relation to the subject. Your energy reflects the way you think. Therefore, if you think negatively, you will remain in negativity.

But, isn't a tragedy of any kind bad or difficult for its victims?

Yes, it is if we disregard the role of illusion. But I can't disregard illusion since I am perfectly aware that everything in the relative world is mixed with illusion. Please accept that truth yourself. The quality of your life will very much depend on accepting that truth. The same applies to the so-called prey and predators. I am getting back to your question about the role of illusion in a tragedy.

A predator resides deep in the illusion of detachment and the illusion of insufficiency. An illusion of detachment is rooted in the predator's mind. It makes him feel distant, chosen, right, and more powerful than a prey he attacks. But, none of that is true. A predator is not separate from his prey, nor better or more powerful. A predator's perception of himself gives him the right to treat the prey the way he does and derives

from complete ignorance and primitive understanding of life. As a result, there is a consequence. Action and reaction. Not ad-hoc punishment and not condemnation. Not a lecture on karma, but a simple and exalted process of consequences. As one sows, so shall one reap, in time.

A predator will become a prey. The prey will become the predator.

A soul that decides to become a predator treats an illusory prey in a particular manner. He will feel the consequences of his choice: By hurting someone else, he hurts himself, too.

The prey need not become a predator in turn, especially in extreme cases ending up in his so-called murder. At the moment of dying, the prey's spirit leaves its body deeply conscious of the entire process, immeasurably more aware than just a moment before, when it was in the flesh. Death is not the end. Death is the continuation of life in some other, higher dimension.

The illusion of insufficiency makes the predator think he will take his prey's life because he believes that there are not enough life prospects, living space, and resources for both of them. But he can't take another life since living is an eternal process. The life was not the body, and death is transition to another form of existence, which is almost always more purposeful and complete than the previous one had been. The predator becomes a true victim of illusion because the prey has moved to a higher state of consciousness.

No one out of the 100,000 or more people in your country was murdered in the way you believe, because death doesn't exist as such. It is a transition to other dimensions of existence. Once you understand that, illusion will have less impact on your decisions, and you won't want to take the role of predator to compensate for something that you already have in abundance. There is so much of everything in your country, Bosnia and Herzegovina, as is the case in every other country around the world. There is nothing missing in what I have birthed. This especially refers to life, living space, and opportunities to make your lives more purposeful. The illusion of insufficiency is blinding but false.

It's not only that there is no need to kill someone in order to make your own life better. Killing is a completely wrong, useless, and eventually self-destructive choice. As you sow, so shall you reap. And if it hurts when you reap, don't curse, but try to understand what made you suffer. The better you understand the causes of your own suffering, the sooner you will be able to eliminate them. Therefore, I keep telling each human being: "I'm here. I am by your side. I love you unconditionally. I have always been yearning for you. Listen to my words and join me in fantastic life." If you decide to take the role of predator, then you will not be able to hear my words and you will get lost in the myriad of illusions that is the source of suffering.

The point of your life is not to suffer, nor are my actions to punish. Stop suffering. Notice illusions. Then LOVE YOUR NEIGHBOR AS YOURSELF, SINCE BY LOVING HIM, YOU LOVE YOURSELF AND SO YOU LOVE ME, TOO.

A great message. A great philosophy. I wish it could reach the hearts of many illusionary victims of the recent war. The tragedy we spoke about had already happened, and it is better to understand it as an illusionary tragedy. Our relatives have not been murdered. Their death is not an end for them, nor should it be for all their surviving loved ones. Predators could not have been real predators. Those wretches had rather lost their way and ended up in an illusionary trap. They will most probably have a hard time getting out of it.

Yet my whispered invitation always vibrates next to their ears. This book, too, is a whisper directed toward the souls of so-called predators. My love is unconditional and limitless. My mercy is limitless. If somebody allows himself to become a victim of illusion and murders or rapes, I give him my endless mercy and show him a fertile seed of love. It is the only path out of the thick forest of illusions where he finds himself. That will be the only way to annul suffering. Yet suffering will fulfill its purpose. It will show that there is still a lot to do to enhance one's interrupted development. You can't escape illusions unless you have understood how they function.

From time to time I send my emissaries. I send messengers,

torchbearers. This book, too, is some of endless light I have always poured on you. Please understand well what is written and thus get closer to yourself. If you become more conscious of yourself, you will become more aware of me, too. As a result, renaissance will be enhanced, love will soar, a new life will commence.

No victims, no predators. You are all my beloved children. Amen.

Amen.

The Only Way

I have an idea for closing the topic about illusory victims and murderers. It is an important, sensitive topic, unfortunately not only in Bosnia and Herzegovina, but globally. The deepest work of illusion is reflected in violence among people. Violence among people reflects the impact of the deepest level of illusion.

Yes. Under the intense, powerful influence of illusion, a human being moves toward one of two extremes, both of which are pointless. He inflicts violence either on himself or on others. Or both.

Violence inflicted on oneself manifests negative autosuggestion. Negative autosuggestion creates fear, anxiety, physical exhaustion, withdrawal, and insecurity, which altogether lead to depression. You will remember, I have already spoken about it.

When a person resorts to violence against other human beings, his mind is ruled by hatred, rage, madness, and inferiority or superiority complexes. It is often the case that one who inflicts violence on others also becomes self-destructive. When you hate someone or deliberately make him suffer, such base emotions infiltrate feelings toward yourself. It is not so difficult to understand, since by hating another you hate yourself. That is a matter of fact because you are all one. Your proposal should be in line with this, and it's going to be a good one.

I think it is. In fact, the question I want to ask you is in line with it. And your answer will be the last word in our discussion of so-called scoundrels and victims.

Continue.

If a child murderer and bereaved mother stood next to each other, what would be the optimum purpose and outcome of their encounter?

A mutual desire to rise above the deep illusions that each, in his or her own way, is under.

Supposing that is what they both want, what might they say, if they spoke at all?

To find truth and rise above their illusions of victim and predator, they would have to tell each other their own truths.

What would that dialogue sound like? Please. Tell me.

Sure.

> **A child murderer and a mother are next to each other.**
> **They are both willing to rise above illusion.**
> **He was a middle-aged man and she was thirty years old at the time when he—in his madness and hatred—took her underage child from her hands and *killed* him in front of her eyes.**
> **Afterward he has become aware of how appalling was the act he had committed.**
> **Even though he seriously doubts the grief-stricken mother will ever forgive him, he will nevertheless try to present to her the state of his soul, which now longs for redemption.**
> **Gathering strength, he slowly raises his face to the mother's swollen, weeping eyes. She shows every mark of bereavement and despair.**
> **For some time, the predator and victim look at each other. He utters the following, barely audible words:**
> **"I beg you to summon strength and hear what I have longed to tell you, have tried badly to say for some time. In fact, I have nothing to offer except a swarm of repentant thoughts from my miserable inner being. Except that you hear them now, I have no other avenue of relief. *I have no***

other way."

In that instant, the mother is overcome with emotion and would escape listening to the murderer. Having acted the way he did, he influenced her destiny. Yet, miraculously a bit of good will opens the door that would bar the executioner. She nods her head almost imperceptibly, sensing that Holy dialogue might repair the irreparable.

Why did you stop this unique presentation so suddenly?

Because now that they have agreed to have a dialogue, you have to give it a title. Their dialogue will open the path to repentance and forgiveness. Forgiveness does not obliterate the hideous deed. But liberation from guilt comes through the healing power of Spirit. All of this is badly needed in your world. Therefore, add that pivotal title now.

Holy Dialogue of Release

"Miserable woman, I caused your suffering. In the worst moment I allowed the illusion of detachment to overwhelm me. I saw you, a woman with ethnicity and skin color different from mine, and was deluded. I feared your child's existence threatened my children's survival—threatened all the children of my ethnicity. At that time, I wasn't aware that I was deeply sunk into the illusion of insufficiency. My goal during the war was to cleanse the space I considered mine of people of other ethnicities and religions. I fell into madness thinking that there was not enough for all of us in this country: not enough food, water, money, or jobs. I sought reasons for my hatred in historical myths that told me how people of your ethnicity weren't worthy to enjoy the bounty and didn't deserve to live. I was blind with fear, barbarity, and madness. I took your child from your arms and murdered him.

"I violated two basic laws of living, doing something I could never endure to be done to me or my family. I opposed my freedom to yours and your family and committed the most heinous crime. I hurt you and killed your child, and when I did it, I wasn't aware that I was hurting myself even more. In the end, I prayed to God—the only One, the God of all of us—to give me a chance to show you my repentance for what I did. Without repentance my life will pass in pointless fear and suffering. I see it clearly now: We are all One. By hurting you, I hurt myself, too. Your forgiveness is the only way my life will have any resolution. Without your forgiveness, I bear the consequence of my crime until the end."

Before saying a word, the mother looks carefully into the penitent's face. She is looking for sincerity. The man does not lower his eyes.

The mother says, "It would be easy to withhold the forgiveness you are asking for. I could nurture desire for revenge, for all the punishment that could be meted out to you, for your execution. You caused my unbearable suffering, and I could wish the worst suffering for you. Many people live deep in their illusions, unable to imagine any other treatment for a person like you, the man who murdered a child.

"However, there is another important question. What is the final point of the fate that touched each of us? You, a murderer; me, mother of a murdered child; my child, murdered at the beginning of his life? If I choose to withhold forgiveness, will I wrap myself in hatred and mental devastation? What might the act of forgiveness give me, and what would it cost me to *not* forgive you?

"You did not ultimately kill my child, as it is impossible to stop life. I am not the mother of a dead child, but the mother of the eternal living force. My baby is not dead. He has only left his bodily form and enjoyed indescribable relief at the moment his wounded body released him. A living spirit, he briefly resided in the body I named my child. Then he left to follow his developmental path to the Absolute. And nobody and nothing could stop him in that Holy intent.

"A murderer is but the blind executor of Providence's choice. Providence is the reflection of a collective consciousness, of an overall spiritual matrix that includes all living humans. We each fulfill the purpose of our existence in our current living forms. The murderer did satisfy his unnatural desire to kill and then he understood that his inherent role can't be to murder, because hurting others hurts himself.

"The murdered child fulfilled his intent to reside but briefly in one body on Earth, and then to leave it on a precisely determined developmental path to the Absolute. I have come to understand a truth: No one can be a murderer or be murdered, since life has its own continuous and unstoppable course. **Therefore, I forgive, even though I know that in the essence of essence I have nothing to forgive the man before me. To continue with his development, he will have to forgive himself.**

"My little baby fulfilled his life purpose on his sky path and after some time, I will learn peace, despite everything."

The woman accepts the man's repentance.

Illusions vanish.

Truth has healed the ignorant injuries.

I Will Become a Wise Man and You Will Become My Wife[10]

Wisdom expressed here should be subject to expert analysis, because our dialogue cuts to the core of a problem that remains unresolved after thousands of years. It is the path to understanding even in the most difficult and conflicted moments. Repentance, forgiveness, and the release that results: These are not empty words. We have forgotten their real meaning, as we have forgotten ourselves. We are lost in a maze of illusions and do not see the way out. How can I inspire people to notice the illusions, to see for themselves the extent we are absorbed in our own illusions?

You will tell them about it in just this way, encouraging them to use their own wisdom. I have been doing it for as long as anyone can remember. Throughout history, all teachers, spiritual masters, and messengers, known and unknown to you, have raised their voices against humans' persisting in illusions. But only a few wanted to hear what they were told, and then the Enlightened were stoned or crucified.

Western contemporary intellectuals exercise ridicule or criticism to prevent the truth from spreading. But I constantly inspire it. They impugn the intentions of enlightened messengers. They praise and endorse insane cultural, philosophical, and political notions crowned by the deepest illusions. They call for actions of conscious, semiconscious, or

10   A song by famous Sarajevo rock composer, Dino Šaran.

unconscious self-destruction. **And the world continues to live miserably in mental illness, wandering through uncharted, material deserts.**

How can one move the sleepy world? What can one do for the truth to triumph over illusions?

At the moment there is not much you can do to change the world.

So, what is the purpose of this dialogue, this book?

Its purpose is to change you, and to encourage others who read this book—sometime, somewhere—to encourage them to change themselves. You have no power over others. You do have power over yourself, and you can encourage others to realize their own power to change themselves, too.

    Not even I change people's psychological structure directly. Doing that would violate the second basic rule of living. The purpose of my action is to encourage people to do it themselves.

Why must they do it themselves? Wouldn't it be easier for you to publicly and explicitly impose the last word of every dialogue?

... and thus to force illusion to stop. I am not the God of power or a bully God. I am God of kind intentions and inviolable freedom. Any act of mine that stopped the process of knowledge through experience would deprive you of freedom and purpose. Freedom is one of the fundamental, life-giving aspects of my creation, and even I cannot violate it.

Is it possible that there is something you find impossible to do?

For me, the only impossible thing is not to be God. Freedom of choice or the possibility to choose is a fundamental right. Without it, no relationship could be established between me as Absolute and you as an inseparable part of that same Absolute.

What kind of relationship can there be between you and me?

If we speak about a strictly spiritual relationship, then it includes happiness, love, passion, knowledge, freedom, and blissfulness. It is an eternal process in the world of the Absolute.

But when a soul resides in the world of the relative, then I am not present in a personal aspect. In the relative world, illusions take my place. Illusions act through three basic atmospheres of Prakrti: through the atmosphere of purposeful action, the atmosphere of purposeless action, and the atmosphere of inaction.

What's what?

Purposeful action is any action a human envisions and consciously performs to accomplish a purpose. Purposeless action is what the human does without knowing the outcome—what he performs ignorantly. Inaction often follows the outcome of an ignorant action. That is, consequences of the second atmosphere (purposelessness) often lead to the third, inaction. Only after a human being experiences the consequences of his own purposeless action, will the freedom of renewed action open up to him again. And so it goes forever until that person departs the world of relative.

And you are waiting for me in the world of the Absolute.

Yes. As I am waiting for you in my heart—through all eternity.

And a Holy relation between us begins in the world of the Absolute.

The Holy relation between us has never ceased. And in the world of the Absolute, it will fully re-expose itself.

"Once, I will become a wise man and you will be my wife ..."

Oh, yes! Through this wonderful verse you express a great desire. You will be my wise man, lover, and adventurer. *You* already are, but for some reasons known to me only, I don't want to *take* you straight away. There is charm in delay; passion grows in expectation; love grows in uncertainty. The path to joy leads through tears. We shall give it a try. We shall go all the way through transcendental pleasures and further and beyond.

But, but …

… until then, I would like us to sing. There will be powerful poetics of lust between us after so much time in the trackless areas of empty worlds, in a nothingness of mental illusions, in the void of useless ideas. And don't worry, it had to be like that and that is the only way, my dear.

Everything had its purpose.

Don't be sad, darling!
Sing instead! Just sing!
Hands up, dance and sing!

I should sing?!

Hands up, dance and sing!

The first song on the CD in the computer?

Yes, that one. It's such a great song. Sing that great song …

You keep quiet every time I call you from the other shore
You keep quiet, keep quiet, keep quiet, the clear water you stir[11]
 While I am singing along with Dino Šaran, I feel as though you are withdrawing, as if you are leaving me, as if you are separating from the conscious part of me, as if our exalted dialogue is being interrupted.

I am not going away. I am not leaving you. I am not separating from your conscious part. I never have, and I will never will. Our relationship is based on more than an internal dialogue. What characterizes it is limitlessness and complete freedom. Freedom, my dear. The energy of our dialogue, this book, tends to shift you to other levels, the levels where illusions, again, exert their influence.

---

11   "Šutiš" by Dino Šaran.

Why? Why is it so? Shouldn't the goal be to escape illusions, not merge with them?

Wisdom uncovers itself in accordance with time, place, and circumstances. The Balkan Peninsula is the place where merging with illusions often turns into various division and deadly conflict. But the Balkans, as with any part of my creation, has the potential to fulfill the purpose of its existence and thus become hallowed ground.

The Balkans is to become hallowed ground?

You are segregating again. Why should the Vatican be blessed ground for some, but the Balkans' cities should not? Why should Mekka and Medina be blessed cities while Belgrade, Zagreb, Sarajevo, Podgorica, Skopje, Priština, and Ljubljana are not? Why would Europe be a continent preferred to Africa? Why would one thing be more or less valuable than another? Why don't you get rid of the divisive state of mind that lands you in constant, tragic conflict?

And finally, isn't the new arrangement of the Balkans for you one of the most sublime dreams?

Well, yes! I can't lie to you. However, if I had to say what I like and what I don't, what I accept in this place and what I don't, I would have to use the writing style typical of the Balkans. I couldn't do it differently. Swearing would be an intrinsic part of the prose and a key stylistic element of the text.

Do you feel that it is the truest way to express your ideas and pursuits in this place where you live?

I think it is.

And I *know* it is. Then, begin by presenting your dream to all who would like to know more about it.

And you would not hold the language against me?

This question of yours reveals that perhaps you don't completely grasp what we have been discussing. Yet, I know you have understood quite a lot. This question reflects your good manners rather than a way to describe the problems

with which you are coming to terms. We are here to break norms, rules, etiquette, and regulations that make the world a miserable, trackless wasteland. We're here to have dreams and to make all our impossible dreams true. You do have a dream, don't you?

You have a dream …

Part 2

I Have a Dream

One year after the last day of my work on this document (July 13, 2007), here I am sitting at my desk again. I have lost inspiration for this text, though I continue to write other works. More accurately, I was working on another part of this book a year ago. I gave it the subtitle *I Have a Dream* and finished it. After ignoring it for a while, I took it up again, reread it, and found it inadequate to the message, the message I have been trying to share with my book *God is a Woman*.

As a result, it seems I'll have to resume the dialogue I entered into, holding it in the same way as in the first part. However, I am not comfortable, because some may consider this book to be a plagiarized version of Neale Donald Walsch's books, both in style and content. Therefore, for others and myself, I will resolve this dilemma in order to unblock my inner mechanism for inspiration. I will resume my work on paper, and it can be evaluated appropriately. In fact, for these several reasons, I want to detach stylistically from the first part of the book, so that I can distance myself from the source of inspiration which riveted me to my chair and made me type this text.

In the meantime, my life has taken a course completely different from writing, philosophy, or theology. I have been engaged in trade and management in many other industries. Perhaps these texts are the only legitimate reason for my existence right now, but I completely forgot that I should encourage my mental and spiritual affinities. I distanced myself from my own self. I forgot that I have been given a gift for writing, thinking, and meditation, all of which sometimes result in extraordinary messages and spiritual declarations that are fairly important—at least for me. I have betrayed my own principles, but I am trying to return to them again. I hope that in some way readers can share the fruits of these messages in their own thoughts and lives. Perhaps they will want to find answers or know more about passages that were unfamiliar or unclear to them.

Now I am trying to reestablish my own relationship with God—or with my true self. I remember so well that my decision to continue this book is not a wholly one-sided, voluntary act. The truth is a bit different.

Once our family business had met all the requirements for sound financial footing with new loans for capital, I was confident that my previously illusive business ideas would finally be realized. At that very moment a series of unexpected depressive/anxiety episodes sidetracked me. I relived the hell of mental illness and repeated the same questions for the thousandth time: Why now, right now, when I am about to achieve financial stability and family prosperity? Right now, when I have overcome phobias that used to paralyze me? Why now, when I am on track toward peace and well-being with my family? Why right now am I falling into trackless darkness and hard-won harmony is destroyed when I least expected it to? In one moment, I was in control, and in the next, my life fell apart.

Have you ever found yourself once, twice, or more times in similar life situations, devastated and unable to respond?

I have no answer. Even though I have been felled by depression, I have found strength and will power to look for answers from God—God the Woman. And so, after quite some time, I am at my desk, trying to write something that deserves to be read.

I write through interruptions. More precisely, I spend days trying to write down my thoughts, and then I lose the whole point. Then I become a different person who has nothing to do with the man who wrote that passage. I become a driver, seller, manager, optimist, pessimist, depressive, euphoric, hero, coward—everything but a writer.

In both jobs and mental states, I try to find myself, to understand myself. I dedicate myself to finding my own life path. I rush forward by force of will and ignore desires that sidetrack me.

As I write, a thought is beginning. Perhaps it can show me how to define myself. Who am I? What should I do and how should I behave in this world? How should I understand the purpose of my own existence? What is my true task? How can I win or surpass my own weaknesses? How can anyone find himself and live a true life?

I don't know how many people in this world ask these questions, but I suspect that they are few.

I live and suffer. I want to live but not to suffer.

A life full of suffering is no good, regardless of whether you have enough money, a partner, children, property, or food and water. Life without suffering would surely open new dimensions of being and fulfillment. New space. Fresh air. Inspired thought, physical strength, and clarity of mind.

If the question is whether we have the right to live without suffering, I am sure we do. At the same time, I wonder how to relate to ourselves and the surrounding world in a natural, compliant way that turns our suffering, regret, and sorrow into happiness, enjoyment, and spiritual well-being. In the end, the key question is "How do we establish a purposeful, inspired, yet functional relationship with God?"

I will try to find an answer through fragments of thought, writing, and internal mandates, writing it down as faithfully and objectively as I can.

So help me God.

El-'Alek[12]

Bismillahir-rahmanir-rahim[13]

Proclaim! (or read!) (starting by) in the name of thy Lord and cherisher, who created (all), created man (human beings), out of a (mere) clot of congealed blood (embryo):

Proclaim! Thy Lord is most bountiful,

He who taught (man) (the use of) the pen (and writing),

Taught man that which he knew not.

And remember, you who write this down and each of you who read, this moment is a blessed moment. Working together we will solve your problems, overcome your fears, reveal answers to your questions, and discover new paths that will take you out of illusion and the maze of ignorance toward enlightenment, power, and wisdom. Be sure of it. It is my promise to you.

It is my promise.

12   A dangling clot—the name of the first Ayats revealed to the Islamic prophet Muhammad, Arabic.

13   In the name of Allah, the Most Compassionate, the Most Merciful, Arabic.

Expansion

With you. I am trying to be with you. I am trying to find a way to stay in constant and functional relationship with you. It is hard to have no original text for doing this, but then I have already written about that.

Plus, there are many other things tormenting me. I don't know how to connect all the dots in my life and take the correct position toward myself and people around me. In fact, it's hard to deal with myself, to tie up loose ends and make things easier. How can I find the functional form of a successful life? What would a *successful life* really be, anyway?

First of all, I welcome you from the bottom of my heart. I am very glad that our communication is being reestablished. This is and will be an original text. Let's solve that concern first. You can relax when it comes to that. You can continue your work as your inspiration, will, and desire arise. I am by your side. I support you and I will be glad to tackle topics of general interest.

It is perfectly clear to you that what we are going to discuss will not be dedicated to you only even though you will benefit from it. So, embark on a new writing adventure with no hesitation or unease. It will do you good, I think. It will be good for you and others, too.

You know what has brought me to the computer.

Yes, I know what has happened.

Is that all part of your plan? I wonder if it is possible that some of our most extremely unpleasant life experiences may be part of God's plan?

Nothing has ever happened that was not subject to my perfect order. Not a single atom of an entire substance, not a single photon, not a single cause and event in what you call the time and space continuum, has ever been or will be out of my control or approval.

Do you suppose that this thought will be comforting when something unspeakable happens to a person? In fact, what can possibly comfort a person experiencing torment of any type?

*First of all***, you should know that nothing** *extremely bad* **has ever happened to anyone. Or in other words, what seems to be** *extremely bad* **for a person at some point is only part of the process that is surely taking him to something extremely good. On the other hand, even though I am the perfect controller of all time and space events, I still don't influence the causes and consequences that affect your lives one way or another. When your life is all pain and suffering, you can be sure that you are experiencing the effect of cause and consequences. That is a reactive life.**

Some would call it the mind at the center of such a reaction. And they are right. In reactive living, any reaction—good or bad—will seem to be something your mind cannot figure out or control. The reaction begins and ends of itself. Yet we are talking about causes and consequences, action and reaction, positive and negative life experiences.

When it comes to positive reactions, there appears to be no problem. You seem to have selected events that strike you as negative. And what do you do? When you get sick, or a loved one dies, a car crashes, poverty endures, or war comes, you fall onto your knees, lose faith and lament, or you react callously to others' suffering.

Yes, exactly, because I don't understand how negative experiences can take us to something *extremely good.*

To start with, take an example from your own life. A quite recent example. Approximately a month ago you experienced

depressive episodes once again.

Yes. It is really embarrassing to think you have recovered from an illness, and then realize it is still there.

I agree. However, the question may be "What caused the relapse?" And it is good that we are talking about that type of mental disease, as many people are dealing with similar ailments, or will soon.

Of course. This could be a very interesting topic. Depression somehow occurs with other diseases of body or mind. I hope this dialogue will help many people gain control of their illness and resume their normal enjoyment of life. However, it is still not clear to me how something negative can turn into something positive. And if it does, why does it become negative again?

Negative and positive are relative terms, especially when they refer to what you call illness. You have already heard that birth, illness, aging, and death are components of life in a relative world and that it is impossible to overcome them without spiritual superstructure. That statement is vital. You have something we'll call *spiritual superstructure*.

Once you temporarily lose connection with the spiritual part, with your own self—and by that I mean *me*—you will experience causes and consequences of living. Those are different—pleasant or not—for each being, depending on the case. If they are pleasant, there will be no development, changes, or reactions to the existing state of affairs. But you already know that.

If you and your family have good health and a good life, you will never want to change. Aware that mere death is at the end of the story, you won't do anything to change things. And then what will you have? A good job, properties, a good partner, healthy and intelligent children, enough free time for recreation, art, and sports, as you may like, and a lot of friends with whom you share nice moments. Youth, middle age, and peaceful old age. Travels and leisure. That's the dream of at least of most people.

So one will ask why God would have anything against such a way of life. And my answer is: I am not in favor of it.

I am even more against such a life for any of you. It is your decision how you will live your life and I have never interfered with any of your decisions.

Making your decisions is a right inherent to you. Deep in your heart, you know that. Therefore, you make decisions and express the freedom inherent to you: freedom to think, decide, and act. The possibility of choice reflects absolute freedom of thinking and acting, and thought is creative. In that sense, you make various decisions and based on them, you create life to be at your disposal as fully as you can.

Freedom is the greatest gift I could have given you. But the choices are yours. The problems (if there can be any problems) arise when your ideas about life translate into your own reality. Your mind generates these ideas at the same time it disregards its own spiritual superstructure. At one moment, and for the reasons that we will deal with at a later stage, all of you find yourselves in spiritual amnesia. You keep forgetting who and what you are, and why you exist the way you exist.

Most people today live in a state of spiritual amnesia. Go into the street and ask someone who he really is. It is unlikely that you will get a straight and correct answer. As a matter of fact, people may think they are this or that—a university professor or laborer, atheist or believer, black or white, male or female, sportsman or artist, Serb or Croat, American or Chinese. I may even think about more diverse characteristics of their personality, but generally, each of these answers will reflect what we have already identified as *spiritual amnesia*. Human beings seem to have gotten lost, they have overlooked the purpose of their existence and undermined the basis of their own spiritual superstructure.

In this state they make what we may conditionally call *wrong decisions.* A bad decision will lead to a bad action. The consequence of the bad action will be a bad reaction. The bad reaction causes pain and suffering. Pain and suffering occur not only as inevitable life events but also to remind you of your bad decision. A wrong decision is a sign of spiritual amnesia.

Pain and suffering, in contrast to happiness and satisfaction, warn us to make some substantial changes within ourselves. By all means, to make a change to reestablish the spiritual superstructure is to make a positive change. Therefore, you can figure out that negative and positive in the context of your life are relative. The constant feeling of happiness and satisfaction, if it occurs in a condition of spiritual amnesia, will never make you think of who you really are and what you are doing in the world.

Who are we really, then, and what is the purpose of our lives in the world we live in?

Before I say it, I would like you to tell me who you think you really are and what the purpose of your life may be.

Should I start from obvious determinations?

Of course. Something like a top-of-mind answer.

Let's say I feel as a human being, a man, white one, Muslim by birth, and pacifist. Perhaps a Bosniak, Mostarian, writer, humanist … Sometimes, I feel like a lowlife. Lately, I find it fairly difficult to take a position regarding myself. For me, the question of one's own definition has become a real dilemma.

All definitions of you that you have mentioned are partly correct. More precisely, one definition is missing, and that is the one that states what you really are.

Well, then, who am I?

You are a spiritual creative being—eternal, immortal, and powerful. The source of your energy is uninterrupted. The well of your blissfulness never runs dry. You are the one who you are. Forever, endlessly.

A spiritual creative being? That's me?

Yes.

And what about all other definitions that you described as *partly correct*?

All those lesser definitions spring from the spiritual amnesia I was talking about. If you consider yourself white, black, mother, father, Catholic, Orthodox, Muslim, Hindu, Jewish,

87

New Yorker, Belgradian or Sarajevan, and at the same time you disregard your true nature as a spiritual being, then you are missing out. You have deleted your power of creation and are living reactively. Spiritual amnesia makes you think that your house is merely yours, your street is merely yours, the nation you belong to as only yours. You trade the endless space you belong to and endless goods you may use for narrow definitions, instead, and then you act accordingly.

That's how misconceptions are created. They lead to irrational prejudices, wrong conclusions, or pointless moves. Much-vaunted bad decisions rise from such limitations as you have imposed on yourself. Wrong decisions precede wrong actions. Wrong actions cause bad reactions. Bad reactions lead directly to your pain and suffering. Depression is the consequence of negative reactions. Everything starts with spiritual amnesia and ends in the state that you define as suffering.

How can I retrieve and affirm my identity as a spiritual and creative being? How can anyone do that? Does it mean that we have to re-define who we are?

With such a question and in such a way you open your mind and reexamine your self identify. As an ethnical person, ask yourself if being ethical makes you really fulfilled and developed. Further, does your being male or female, red or yellow, a communist, socialist, or capitalist, father, child, or mother, a believer or an atheist, nationalist or pacifist, really make you a happy and complete being?

Reexamine your identities over and over. Search for an answer that is deep in your heart. If you feel that one of your mentioned or unmentioned commitments make you fulfilled and happy, then don't search for esoteric truths. Stay where you are in the place that suits you until you decide differently. If you feel that your identities are not what you want yourself to be, or what you sense deep in your heart, then start waking up as a creative spiritual creature.

I say to all, re-create yourselves into what you have always been. Become Gods, light carriers, and supporters of truth. Truth will prevent evil from overpowering good; the darkness, light; and illusion, knowledge. I am here to help you in such a rising process. As a mother, father, brother, or sister, from times beyond memory and forever.

I have to admit this is quite inspirational. What's more, it is large. However, I think that the challenge is in concrete implementation. I suppose that many other people have the same problem. So, how to realize the truth in everyday life?

I recognize that many peoples have read the wide range of books about spiritual truth. They accept the knowledge and wisdom they find. Despite those "manuals," they seem unable to find themselves or achieve something right.

Yes, it's true. At least, when it comes to me, it is true.

First, you should expect that a transcendental process may include what is called "The Dark Night of the Soul." It's a depression of soul, exhaustion of body, and confusion of mind. It often occurs between discovering that you've had enough of material pleasures and while you are still looking for the spiritual joy ahead. It's a boundary, a vacuum.

Many who are reading this now (including you, my dear, as you write it down) know what I am talking about. But not all know how to get out of such a state. How can one overcome the dark night of the soul and turn it into something more like the moonlit night of inner peace and spiritual bliss?

The point is that you must not resist such a state. Your mind, body, intelligence, and soul (all that you are) will take you where you belong at any given point. You have endless opportunities to overcome the dark side of your spirit. Feel free to give yourself up to any of them. Never reject anything within yourself.

Some seekers will return to the covering wing of mundane experiences and continue to find meaning and purpose in their existence there. Some will achieve spiritual bliss and reach the other side of the line between the relative and the absolute. Some will combine all these findings.

It is important not to stay in the same place, but to set a goal toward which you can coordinate your spirit, intelligence, mind, and body. Disharmony among these four components

interrupts life's rhythm. It skews energy and makes you susceptible to a range of diseases.

And if you are not sure where you really want to go, then hold on for a moment and listen for your very true essence. It will reenforce all four parts of your being simultaneously. You will recognize that voice by the message it carries. For you, it will signal peace and tranquility. It will carry reliable instruction for steering your life boat. Hear it, regardless of the message, and soon you will realize that the next decision you made took you from the darkness to light, into a new experience that you never suspected.

Even if you don't recognize that message straight away, don't panic, don't curse. Your healing spirit will be gently persistent and certainly sufficient to guide you out of your dead-end street. Then stop every now and then and look for your inner peace. Soon you will find it, and it will surely take you out of darkness and show you the way toward a new world that you were completely unaware of—a new world, new experiences, and airy regions.

That is the purpose of *the dark night of the soul*: to rediscover light, realize over and over again how much power has been given you, you who are a part of me. Together we create something from nothing and trade depression for production. Use powers given to you, reach for them even when you doubt they are available, and they will be there for you just as surely as dawn rises red after a long, opaque night, or as a clear, starry sky rises over the parched Earth.

It's my promise. It's your destiny. Give yourself up to it and the knowledge you gain will turn into working wisdom.

There is something else you should know. Wisdom does not reside in books; wisdom resides in you. Don't look for truth only in books. Books can show you where to go but will not replace the journey. Also search and re-search your mind and the power of your spirit. A truth will turn up suddenly in front of you, and it will be so clear and powerful that you will never again deny its existence.

On the other hand, it's easier to find the right path if you follow the instructions I am giving. And thus the circle becomes complete—not for you to keep going nowhere, but to create more and more new circles of life that are wonderful and limitless, all-permeating and active, lifting and transcendental.

And now, for the sake of easier understanding, we can sum up.

First, you have a *life*, that fantastic, enlarging process of limitless existence. But due to *spiritual amnesia*, which comes along at some point in life, you wrongly identify with *outside identities*, and subsequently make *wrong decisions*. Wrong choices lead to *wrong actions* toward someone or something; *wrong actions* create unexpectedly bad reactions, which directly cause *suffering and pain*. Suffering and pain remind you that there is something in your way of thinking and acting that goes against who you really are. It is then wise to ask yourself what it would be to rediscover the truth and act again in accordance with it. In that way, you will overcome suffering, and truth will be clear to your mind and body. The soul has always been found right next to truth. Your soul has always known all about everything because a super soul is next to it. And that super soul is a localized aspect of me in you. Feel its pulse, and adjust your life rhythm to it. It's a process of rediscovering what you are, what you have always been, and what you will always be.

And now the other side. How can one understand life if one has not experienced the negation of life? Or know what it means to be spiritual if one never identified with what is only material? Or value pleasure without suffering pain? I don't trust that we can be wise if our wisdom has never been overshadowed by madness or confusion.

Exactly. Just as you have said it. You've got it now. You can move on.

You live in the relativity of duality so you can understand the Absolute One. You are the truth, but to understand the truth, which you are, you have to experience everything that you are not.

From truth's point of view, it appears as it is *not* because only if you understand a lie which is the truth, can you accept the truth which is truth indeed.

Therefore, don't condemn suffering, don't condemn pain or yourself for being in pain. Circumstances have brought you to a horrible place that is not your final destination. You can be certain of that. It's a place where you will have to stop, call out your true self, and call upon my true self. Then you can open the door to new spaces that will take you away from the mess you are in. I am here to help you. I am here to strengthen you each time you think you don't have it yet or can ever have it. I have no other purpose of existence except to be by your side when you call my name. In times of suffering and inconvenience I'm here. I am here when you forget about me in times of happiness and pleasure. I am always at your side. I have always been and will always be. There is not the minutest fraction of time when matters are not so.

Al-Inshirah

Bismillahir-rahmanir-rahim

Did we not open your heart for you

And relieve you of your burden,

which [almost] broke your back?

Did we not exalt your name?

Indeed ease accompanies hardship.

Indeed ease accompanies hardship.

So when you are free from [your obligations], strive hard [to worship God]

and turn eagerly to your Lord.

Amen

I Stopped Fighting: I Think That Is How Wisdom Starts[14]

Oh, my dear, I think the guidance you have given me is producing some results in my life. I am getting some new ideas and am animated by a new will. It seems that a deadlock is being resolved. I have a goal. I have an idea—an idea to follow.

Then on second thought, I am not sure what my real and true motive for working on this book may be. I am not even sure what to call this manuscript. Is my goal money? Fame? Enlightenment? Help with awakening others?

I am still having a nightmare. Life, money, love, relationships, God and me, me and God, people, streets, cities, a planet, a universe, the meaning of all of these …

The meaning. I see that the search for meaning has brought you before me. Meaning is a word or notion which incorporates many things—all things, I would say.

Life encompasses all forms of mega-existential existence; meaning is a code for the living to use in order to act kindly, beneficially. And everything is living. There is nothing that is not alive and active in the endless space and time I keep on a tiny piece of my infinite, transcendental body.

If, while living your life, you find yourself on the path of kind action, then you will feel your life pulsating in accordance with the universe. You are happy, fulfilled, you feel and live

14   A verse by Branimir Štulić, a composer and writer.

your true self in unity with me. Thus, you are unified with everything that exists and the purpose of your existence is fulfilled, but fulfilled does not mean it is completed. Never completed. What you call life—existence, searching, reaching, and fulfillment—never ends. Nothing will ever finish, stop, or terminate. My world is one of expansion and transformation; it is a world of pulsing contraction and expansion. My world has neither a beginning nor an end. My principles do not recognize any static quality. Everything is created without being created; everything dies and never ceases to exist.

My principles do not recognize any static state. Everything is created without being created; everything dies without ceasing to exist.

That sounds nice, but a bit worrisome. Is it possible that fighting never stops? Isn't there something we call the rest of the soul and the peace of the spirit?

When you stop fighting, you will automatically find peace of the soul. You fight with something or someone because you don't understand the essence of attack or defense. There is no need to fight at all. For you, such a statement may sound confusing, but I will say it again: THERE IS NO NEED TO FIGHT FOR SOMETHING OR AGAINST ANYTHING.

I will be honest with you. This claim is not only confusing, but it would be impossible to realize. How do you not fight against someone who openly and deliberately attacks you? How can you not defend yourself without putting your life, health, and material goods in jeopardy? I lived through the war. I know very well how it works when someone attacks to hurt you, kill you, eliminate your kind, and take away what belongs to you. And he's doing all for nebulous reasons of his own.

I have never thought of somebody else's house as mine. Obviously, there used to be many who thought of my house as theirs. They also devalued my life and the lives of my family. Regardless of all the political connotations and ethnic clashes still at play in my town, Mostar, I know perfectly well what I went through from 1992 to 1995.

Do you suppose I don't know about that war? Do you really think I have not witnessed every war waged on the planet from as long as anyone can remember?

Of course you have seen what we have endured. Therefore, the following question is legitimate: How can there be no reason to fight when we are so frequently the victims of malicious attack? Even other species—plants, insects, animals—attack us under various circumstances. In the most drastic cases, other people try to kill us. We are often forced to fight. Whether we want it or not, fighting for survival is a necessary part of our lives. You can't deny it.

It's a complex problem, so try hard to understand what I am going to emphasize to others through you. You know, you are not such a weak medium as you may think. Don't underestimate yourself. Be aware of your value; appreciate and accept it. Honesty is your virtue. Your honesty is the characteristic that best opens you up to me. You are still not aware of the paths you are about to take with me. An adventure is about to start.

You don't have to fight to get things underway. Now, I will explain why this is so.

The problem is complex. Yet the problem doesn't really exist. You might call an uncomfortable psychological state or life situation a problem if you don't see a quick way to overcome such an unfavorable state of affairs. Then, you resort to what you call a fight.

Fights can be long or short, meaningful or meaningless, with certain or uncertain outcomes. In its simplest definition a fight is your defense of whatever you consider yours because it is vulnerable. Remember: vulnerable. If it is vulnerable, then it is fragile and powerless. It can disappear or be destroyed. You would fight to protect something weak like that, something you could lose forever, something that can be taken away from you. This might be your life and health, your family's life and health, or your goods and property.

But, in essence, there is nothing that can be destroyed, as everything is indestructible. There is nothing we can lose, as we have everything in abundance. Nothing can be taken from

you since you are completely and infinitely content. Therefore, if you are ready to fight someone in order to protect someone or thing, then transform your motivation to fight into the nonsense of defending someone whom it would be impossible to lose. Even in the worst scenario, loss is impossible in the world I created.

If in that fight to defend, your loved one or your property appear to be lost, remember that no one has ever destroyed or exterminated anything, as the energy of all creation is constantly being transformed. Therefore, nobody can kill or hurt your body, which is spiritual, endless, and indestructible. You will know it automatically if you die in a so-called fight. No one has ever killed another person. Life cannot be lost.

Explanations and opinions that are not in line with what I have just said are untrue. There is no need for a fight. It isn't necessary. But if you fight for something, expect your fighting experience to take you through to a comprehensive experience of life without violent conflict.

Yet, you cannot fully perceive the meaning of life without violence, until at some point you have held the incorrect view that fighting is inevitable. It is an irony.

Exactly. You understand. You comprehend. You are getting closer to your own inner self. You are also getting closer to me, within you. In accordance with your current state and position, you are climbing out of the mud of embarrassment.

But I had to recognize that mud of embarrassment so I could understand the life to come in an ocean of comfort.

Yes. In the ocean of comfort, floating in the boat of knowledge and happiness, with God as the skipper.

Oh, I live for that day, for that moment, for that time. I have had enough of life in relativity and misconception. I am ready to take off into new space, into absolute, immense, and fulfilling spheres. You are the female skipper and crew. Please bring that moment as soon as possible. Answer my prayers. Make it happen.

My dear, it already has.

What do you mean? You are confusing me again. You scare me. As I said, my emotions are moving toward something different, better. It's good they are moving even a little after the stagnation of my recent depression. Nevertheless, I am not yet on the Awareness and Happiness boat with you, sailing in the ocean of comfort.

And I keep telling you that you are; that's exactly where you are, but in your space-time continuum you still don't feel it. Things are taking place here and now. Everything happens in one endless time explosion that is expanding to all of space, all the way to infinity. You choose existence through various fragments and a single time zone that is not linear, even though you may have the impression it is. When you replace the feeling of linearity in time and space with an experience of a single but infinite *here and now*, with all its infinite variations, you will conclude that time in the sense of past and future does not exist. There is only one all-permeating instant, the other side of *here and now*, which, depending on circumstances, you live through in ways you choose.

I will try to reason in a way that would be easier for me to understand. I have become aware of myself, but that awareness has yet to come into my life.

As though you are waiting for a train at the station, you have your ticket. The approaching locomotive is vibrating the platform. The train is stopping. Passengers get off; others get on. In the next moment, you are on the train and heading to your destination. Remember, just remember that up until a few minutes earlier you were at the station. Soon, you will reach the town you are traveling to. You will get off at that station and be at your destination.

First, you wait for the train, you get on, you travel, and then get off. Past, present, future. Both past and future push into the present, as present is the only moment we live with it. Everything else is an illusion. Time is stopped; you keep moving through it. Time doesn't fly. Time is always standing, static, stuck in its constant present. You move through time. You travel through time just as you move through space. You are a time and space passenger on the time-space road

stretching through the endless and unclear layout of Here and Now.

So simple and clear an explanation of time and space. So far I have not understood it in this way. Now, however, I am able to see how simple the process is that was difficult to understand until now.

I have a confession to make. You are amazing. So smart. I have never had such a healing dialogue. Certainly, I am talking to God/Goddess and that fact in itself has extraordinary meaning. I will be honest with you. I am trying to imagine you as a breathtakingly beautiful woman who walks with me along a sandy beach on an exotic island at sunset. We walk, touch, speak, look at each other, are quiet and then we talk again. Word by word. Step by step. Touch by touch. A red, setting sun. Palm trees and coconut trees. Spacious, powerful ocean. Your hair waves loose with the wind, and here is the beautiful, serene face of the woman who is Goddess. That's how I imagine it.

God is Woman.

Your words shatter illusion in the same way as sun clears the morning fog. "Your hands are mother, your body is a fairy tale— that's how I know you."[15] Your mildness touches my soul the way a soul touches freshly washed skin. Your timbre surpasses gentleness with the sound of waves that break one after another on endless, sandy beaches. Your lotus-flower footprints in the sand make me dizzy with lust. When I look in your eyes, I would faint. But with an enormous effort I stay conscious to watch the beauty and listen to the wisdom. None of it is enough for me.

That's how I see things. I don't see any other point in living except to come to a dimension where my fantasies are real.

Thinking is a creative act. I promise it will be like that, and even wilder, stranger. There is no way to demonstrate, using your limited language, how much more fantastic it will be. Soon you will be back home where I am fervently waiting for you. You have been away for quite some time. You will soon be back to your God. I am your wife.

Each person participating in the creation of this book (all the people looking at it now are its coauthors because their

---

15   "Fantazija," by Branimir Štulić.

99

desire contributed to the creation of this book) should know that they are free to realize me in their hearts as a Woman God—their Goddess. You may disregard theology and religions, imams, rabbis, gurus, friars, catholic and orthodox priests. They will curse this text and its messages. All of you who have longed for fresh spiritual confirmation take a step forward toward me, and I will leap whatever is between us. I will be close to you and embrace you with unconditional love. In my world there is no sorrow or pain. In my world even relativity is absolute. Each word is a song, each move is a dance. Join me in achieving a sense of complete life. Love is your destiny and mine. Love is when fulfillment and enjoyment start.

Angry with God

I am having a bad day, I can't share details. I can't speak about details as I am not sure I have the consent of a person I am in a conflict with to write more about it. Full discretion must be guarded; full disclosure is not guaranteed.

You should respect that person's decision. Respect any decision by a person related to you.

But I have to tell you something about it. I am boiling in constant emotional derangement. You speak about life in cycles, about suffering and happiness, pleasures and pain, darkness and light. But I am tired of duality. I think I have had enough bad experiences; there is no need for me to suffer any more, fear, be disappointed, cry, or shake. I don't need it. Nevertheless, bad things keep happening to me.

Then change your point of view and the way you see events that appear to have a negative impact.

How? How can I do it?

Well, simply by changing ...

Stop! Hold on! It sounds so simple when you say it. I have been trying to keep things simple, but complications keep arriving, just like uninvited, unwelcome guests.

All right. I don't know how to start my explanation without irritating you.

There you are! Is it possible that there is something that God isn't aware of?! Because that's how I feel right now. You really seem not to know when to put an end to insane happenings and conditions in your world. If you did, things would be different. It would be better. Bad things would end soon.

What can you tell me right now when I am full of bitterness, rage, fear, and depression. This happened to me when I expected my life to change for the better, and when the time has finally come for positive developments. You also promised to me that better times for me and my family were on the horizon. Are your promises realistic, or your truth questionable?

My promises are realistic, my dear, and my truths are un-

changed ...

Hold it, hold it! Give me some other, more constructive solution. Get personally involved in my life and do it right now. Let it happen now. Let me feel now that your kindness is unconditional and your love endless. Do it. Do it now. Right now! Make it easy for me.

It is too tough. "Who is going to write all these words when it gets too tough?"

I am waiting.

I am waiting.

Seconds and minutes pass. Hours, days, years will pass. You will not be by my side. I will not be by your side. Derangement.

So, who is going to sing all these songs when it gets tough, you fool?

Can I tell you something? I will make it short and then we will see how to move on.

Of course you can. Tell me anything as long as it isn't the way the things are.

How about postponing your work on this book, taking a pill, separating yourself by going to another room, going to bed. Try disregarding bad vibrations coming from your mind and opening up to positive ones. Do that very carefully.

Forget about me—even though I never forget about you— if it will be easier for you that way. If you want, disregard that I never forget about you. Try not to think about anything

else but what makes you comfortable. From a distant part of your mind, take out impressions that comfort you. Don't bother with which pictures, thoughts, or fantasies you have. Whatever comforts is good.

Listen to me. Postpone everything and get a rest. Even if you are angry at me or hate me, don't fight these feelings. Let them last as long as it takes, and they will leave just as they came. If you are angry or hateful toward other people or yourself, the winning formula is the same. The winning formula is always the same. Stop suppressing your feelings. Don't fight them. Don't resist them. Opposing them helps them persist. You have already heard that.

When you feel you can and want to do it, go out and wash your car. Clean the yard. Do any daily task. Work does not create the man, but there is no man without work. Work heals if it is a task that makes you feel better. Events come in cycles. You will learn to live with duality up to that moment when you don't care anymore, up to that moment when you become a truly wise man. Bad things will come to an end then …

But, we have had enough of that for now. Turn off your computer. Go into seclusion. Find the most appropriate way to calm down and let the day pass. And it will pass as any other. Time works for you. I am on your side. Everything is on your side. Believe me. I never lie. Victory guaranteed.

Singlediversity

It's been a few days since I last worked at my computer. I was on vacation. Sea, sun, people, and beaches. I stayed in an apartment with a sea-facing terrace. There, looking toward the sea and breathing pine-scented air, it came to my mind that I would like to write for a living.

I was fighting with a lot of bad thoughts. However, that lifesaving idea somehow survived. To write for a living, and not to ignore all forms of literature except those referring to you, to me, and to all the people I saw from that house on the coast—and in the end, people in the whole world. To write for a living and my work. Then I will profit big by it. Is it good? Is it correct?

I don't see why you would think that I—owning all the wealth of the world—would begrudge your sharing wealth with others. Likewise, I don't see why I—the One who manipulates the energies the way I want—would be against someone's doing what he likes. Therefore, in a chaos that you cannot always control, you are free to choose the path you want to follow. It is your inherent right. I don't have anything to do with it, except for helping you achieve it.

I should replace the word "right" with "choice." That's a much closer meaning. You make your choices, but you don't exercise your rights. Your decision to do something means that, out of endless possibilities, you chose one you consider best for you. If someone gives you the right to something, he can deprive you of that and other rights, too. In such a system, you may exercise or abuse rights or regulations.

Your state systems are developed with rights and

prohibitions. The world you created curtails freedom of thought and action in all possible ways. This includes more or less all current states and systems on your planet.

On the other hand, in the world I offer, you are free to make decisions about your life. You are free to work to make them come true. You and everyone else are free to do it. You all have rights to choose all the time. You can choose anything. Enjoy the freedom I have given you.

The way you speak and I write looks much more like anarchy than a legally regulated system. If everyone acted as he pleased, I doubt everyone would be completely fair to other people.

They would if they'd implement the two basic rules of living. Remember the first two basic rules of living I told you about in the first part of this book. To repeat:

1. DON'T DO TO OTHERS WHAT YOU DON'T WANT DONE TO YOU.
2. YOUR FREEDOM ENDS WHERE ANOTHER LIVING CREATURE'S BEGINS.

Repeat them to yourself and to others. All rules and regulations can be classified into these two basic principles of mutual relations. They point to one truth: WE ARE ALL ONE.

There is no need to write a number of laws, articles, and amendments, which then become pointless. You have lost faith in yourself and everything around you to such an extent that you keep trying to protect your right to life and property by passing a string of laws that often don't function as intended.

In constant strains and squabbles you—and I speak to you collectively—have lost the purpose of your own existence. You see others as opponents, competitors, enemies, foreigners, or nonbelievers. You expect some threat, danger, and an evil from them. The way you see others is a distorted reflection of your own prejudices, because you have not understood yourselves as creative spiritual creatures. Free creatures. Inviolable creatures. Powerful creatures. Realize that you are spiritual and not material, creative and not standardized, free and not limited, powerful and not vulnerable. Then you will be able to understand yourself and everyone around you. You will understand that we are all One, and you will also appreciate the differences I have enriched you with. We are all ONE, but we are all DIFFERENT. We are all SINGLEDIVERSE. The sense of purpose lies in singleness; wealth lies in diversity. You should know that. You are each singlediverse in relation to all other people around you, all individuals, all living beings, so-called living and dead matter around you. Therefore, get up and feel your single individuality from everything around you. Isolate yourself and feel your own specific character, your distinction, a unique code of characteristics typical of you. Use them for your own fulfillment. Once you manage to fulfill yourself, you will fulfill others who touch you one way or another. When you finally understand yourself, others whom you touch will also see a clearer path to their insight and self-realization.

Other light carriers shed light on the darkness when you couldn't find your way out. Your torch, once you light it, will show others the way out of dark labyrinths in their lives. You have recently read the following: "It's better to light a candle than to curse the darkness." So let this book be the candle and the guide.

If you would like writing to be your work, then make your work purposeful, charitable, loving, and knowledgeable. Make it useful and profitable, too. If you rely on me, I will guarantee that things will be as they should.

All things happen in their own way. Therefore, don't curse circumstances; don't curse darkness, suffering, pain, depression, anxiety, powerlessness, poverty, or disease. Everything happens at the perfect time. You experience things at the time, place, and under circumstances that are perfect for the process of your awaking and confirming yourself. Everything is under my supervision, and everything is under your supervision, even when you don't see it that way.

At times when things get out of control, the system falls apart, and life loses meaning, take matters into your own hands. But never do it with your mental or physical power, because neither your mind nor body is conditioned to help the spirit that is the essence of who you really are. Your brain is the tool you will reach out for. It is a link among mind, body, and spirit. Your intellect will never put you on the wrong path or a sidetrack.

Follow instructions from your brain and you will be on the path to creative, spiritual self-realization. That's my path. That's your path. The text of this book follows the light of spotless brains that offer techniques you are about to master.

And that's good. You still need to realize yourself in a spiritual-creative sense. (Once you do it, the universe will burst in front of your eyes with me in the center of everything.) But for now you sense three diverse, but still coherent parts making up the whole of yourself. You are aware of body-mind with its five senses, plus brain and spirit. Sometimes you suffer from poor body- and mind-related impressions. However, your brain is there to get you out of the abyss your body and your mind frantically threw you into.

Therefore, I repeat:

DON'T DO TO OTHERS WHAT YOU DON'T WANT DONE TO YOU.

YOUR FREEDOM ENDS WHERE ANOTHER LIVING CREATURE'S FREEDOM BEGINS.

WE ARE ALL ONE, BUT WE VARY WIDELY. WE ARE ALL SINGLEDIVERSE.

IN A CONDITIONED OR UNCONDITIONED STATE, YOU ARE A COMPLEX OF MIND-BODY AND FIVE SENSES, BRAINS AND A SPIRIT, WHICH IS YOUR ULTIMATE SOURCE OF INEXHAUSTIBLE ENERGY.

IN A CONDITIONED STATE, A REACTIVE MIND IS THE CENTER OF UNPURPOSEFUL ACTIONS.

IN A CONDITIONED STATE, THE BRAIN CAN LINK A REACTIVE MIND-BODY AND A CREATIVE SPIRIT.

THE BRAIN IS A TOOL AVAILABLE TO ALL HUMAN

BEINGS TO TURN THEM INTO SPIRITUAL-CREATIVE PEOPLE. THROUGH THAT PROCESS THEY WILL UNDERSTAND THEMSELVES AS WELL AS THE WORLD AROUND THEM.

IN A REALIZED STATE OF SPIRIT CONSCIOUNESS, A BODY WITH FIVE SENSES AND A MIND MOVES FROM A REACTIVE TO A CREATIVE PHASE.

In short, it's a process. Grasp, adopt, apply it, and the purpose of your existence will be fulfilled.

It seems as if I gave a number of responses to a single question. Sometimes, one answer can be enough for a number of questions.

Therefore, do whatever you think is best now.

Raised, inspiring feelings represent a language that your soul is using to address you through your brain.

I have thought …

Why did you stop? Tell me what you think is best to do at this moment.

Well, then! I think it's best to work on this book as much as I can, to open up to you, to … I know it now! Activate my brain and thus try to tame the scared mind, which has gone mad.

You were thinking while looking at the sea, sky, and clouds from the terrace of your vacation apartment. Which of your many different ideas were closest to the vision of what you want to be, to do, or experience as a human?

A thought that I am healthy in my mind, body, and spirit. I will write about universal and spiritual truths but in a specific and new way, to become … so that I become …

Keep talking. Why did you stop?

I don't know. Perhaps I don't believe the most sublime vision of my own self can be realized. Perhaps I'm not strong enough, worthy enough, to achieve such a goal. That might be the reason.

Regardless of how you think you feel, please go on pronouncing what you would like to be and what you are. Do it that way. There is nothing bad or less worthy in it. Tell me what you think about and hope for, and I will make your most sublime, impossible thoughts come true.

Well, I'll say it! I would like to become a book author known worldwide. I will work hard to make sure this text, once it's ready, is translated into English so then I can send it to world-renowned publishers. I would like everything that has been and will be written here to reach as many people as possible around the world. Then they can use it in their everyday lives.

Great! Is there something else you would like?

I would like to make a profit on it and use the money in the best possible way.

What would be the best way to use it?

I would like to clear outstanding debts. I have been unable to repay them no matter how hard I work. I would like to buy land near the Mediterranean, perhaps close to the Adriatic Sea and build a dream home, where I could work, socialize, and meditate. I would like to initiate the idea of singlediverse as the organizing principle for economic, political, interethnic, and interreligious efforts globally. It would grow in solid opposition to inhuman globalization, to narrow-minded exclusion and religious fanaticism. I would like to fulfill my own life, the lives of my family, but also to change the world. At the age of thirty-four I have the illusion that I can change the world.

I wouldn't agree with you.

How come? Why?

At the age of thirty-four you are just starting to develop a thought (not an illusion, but a thought) that you can change the world.

Oh! This is all too surreal, phantasmagorically surreal.

Things are not as they seem to you, because as they end, all things take on different forms from the ones they will

eventually receive. List your priorities, maybe even in this book, and then, we will follow things as they unfold. There will be some big changes. Start from yourself, and then we will move ahead step by step.

An idea about a SINGLEDIVERSE approach to personal and global problems has arisen. Let's devote our attention to that. This book will be a significant factor in creating a NEW WORLD ASSOCIATION. Not an ORDER but an ASSOCIATION. Not through global, inhuman economic utility, or nationalistic or religious division, but in the NEW WORLD ASSOCIATION. We will use no military or economic force, fear, segregation, or fanatic motivation. We will use peace, love, and patience. Peace, because unrest and chaos stymy creativity; love, because we are sure that hatred and intolerance yield stupidity and lifelessness; patience, because each process toward a better state has its ups and downs, perfectly ordered in cycles and leading to final success.

Therefore, declare before yourself and everyone that the renaissance, the time of waking up and progress, the time of complete unity and celebration of diversity has come.

You have said so many things that I could not have dreamt of until now.

I am She who I am.

Alpha and Omega.

The beginning and the end.

Endless and beyond.

I am and I will be.

You are and you will be.

We are and we will be.

All of you,

All of us,

We all are and we will be,

One and diverse.

Meditative Thoughts

I have been drinking.

I know.

I have been drinking, but I don't think I'm drunk.

You suppose I am drunk.

I don't suppose; I know.

And what do you know about this evening?

I know you are drunk.

Do you condemn this condition?

What condition?

Being drunk.

I don't condemn anything. I propose, characterize, and conclude. I do not condemn. That is not my way, not my nature. That is not who I am.

What is your conclusion then, your proposal or characterization?

Nothing you expect from me. I will neither support nor condemn your decision to have a glass in your hand tonight, to be in company you like, listening to music you enjoy, and listening to jokes that make you laugh.

I had to. It made me feel good. I relaxed. It is all part of life, I guess: rhythm, dance, jokes, gestures, conversation, fooling around. What am I supposed to do? Where does intoxication take me if I continue drinking? Is there some point to living with a glass in the hand?

I repeat: It's your decision, not mine. You decide what you will do with your life and how you will spend the time you are alive. It is you deciding about it, not me. What else would you expect me to tell you? Each of my judgments excludes you as a decision-making body. That would not make sense. Your life amounts to your decisions. It's simple. You are the decision maker, not me. Alcohol, drugs, yoga, eating, walking, sport, art—those are all ways of expressing yourself, your attempts to be clearly heard.

So you are not suggesting anything. You are not pointing to anything?

I am suggesting and pointing, but the final decision is yours.

What are you proposing, what are you pointing to, regarding this evening's event?

I suggest that you not be addicted to anything, not to alcohol, drugs, gluttony, or gambling. Your dependence on a substance would indicate that you have not realized the independent personality I created as you.

I put all the components for enjoyment of life in you, so there is no need for further stimuli. We live to enjoy, and there is no need for external ingredients to enjoy life. The chemistry of enjoyment is already in you, in your tissue, your aura, your creative mind and senses.

The mind is an emotional treasury from which emotions go to the rest of the body by the nervous system. You can be happy with your head, hands, legs, chest, and back. You can be completely happy without any external tool that would come to you. You have experienced this in sexual intercourse. Sex is a natural way of achieving happiness of body and mind. Music that you enjoy so much can also be extraordinary for boosting happiness. Wherever and whenever you can, enjoy life in natural ways. Sex, music, kissing, caressing, sport, caring for plants and animals, helping the powerless and sick. All of that can make you happy, just as philosophizing does. Creativity—painting, composing, labor (one of the

most noble and at the same time devalued human activities), writing, traveling, games, and dancing. There are many ways to enhance happiness and satisfaction.

Sometimes you achieve it by meditating on me. That is an extraordinary way to be happy because it includes all the modes I've mentioned and more.

Meditating on you.

Yes.

Very interesting. How can I meditate on you? Please explain to me explicitly, so I can achieve that level of mental activity.

It's simple. Very simple. What God would I be if I complicated my relationship with you, her, him, or anyone? A path to me is not complicated. It is simple and sublime. A path to me takes you higher and further in the fulfillment of the most sublime, endless vision.

There is no way for you to comprehend me completely, but there are numerous paths to meeting me again and again, encountering the more and more magnificent forms of what I am. And I am All and Nothing. I am Nothing because without nothing there would be no Something or Everything. I am Everything. You can't imagine, see, or realize anything that I haven't been. How, then, could meditation on me be difficult?

The possibilities for touching me are endless, and yet there is no way to comprehend me completely. I am impossible to comprehend. I myself am unable to do it. My energies, in their every diverse form, are pulsating and expanding through limitless reaches of space and time. Wherever you look, whatever you touch, wherever you go, whatever you experience, is all one of the endless manifestations of me. I Am, even when you are oblivious to me, because "memories, knowledge, and oblivion come from me."[16]

So in the end, whatever we do, whatever we think about, whichever way we behave, it comes down conclusively to meditation on you.

Yes, if you believe it to be. Because if you don't, then you will

16   Statement of God in Bhagavad Gita 15.15.

114

be dreaming up different types of mere work and acting on them. Then you will most probably feel as though you are not making progress or that you take one step forward and two steps back.

If you live and work unaware of me as the center of all activity, then sooner or later you will experience futility, the absurdity of existence, fatigue, and numbness. Perhaps all of them together. The longer and deeper you are without me, the narrower your vision, the weaker your influence. By losing me, you will lose yourself, too.

There are no conditions to meet before you follow me. It will suffice to follow yourself because by following yourself, you will inevitably come to me. That will come about not through circumstances, but because inevitably it is the way it should be. Once you lose me/yourself as the pillar of your existence and actions, you will need motivations, and you will think them up.

You create ethnicity and by being loyal to an ethnicity, you will think you are being loyal to me. You create religions and through loyalty to your religion, you expect to show loyalty to me. Nevertheless, there is only one truth, and it is unchangeable. I emphasize it for all of you who find inspiration in this message:

1. DO NOT LOOK FOR ME ONLY THROUGH YOUR OWN RELIGION.

2. DO NOT CONSIDER IT TO BE MY PATH WHEN YOU ARE ONLY FOLLOWING YOUR NARROW NATIONALISTIC IMPULSES.

3. I AM NOT FOUND IN ONLY ONE RELIGION. MY MESSAGE HAS NOT BEEN GIVEN EXCLUSIVELY TO ANY ONE RELIGION, ANY ONE NATION.

Likewise, I am not a member of any particular political party, state system, military power, city, local community, street, or house. I am simultaneously in all of the above. But I am also

out of all your associations and social creations of any century.

Now I don't understand. Is it both possible and impossible to find you through community, nations, and religions?

If you identify with your nation, religion, or armed services and support them in domination over other nations, religions, or militaries, then you are not on the path toward me. What you call segregation, Nazism, military fanaticism, exploitation, or oppression of others is not a path to you, either.

But if you recognize a person of different ethnicity, race, or religion and see the possibility for mutual growth and fulfillment, then I will be present in your relationship. And your association will also be a form of meditation on me. You will discover me whether you are a businessman or a soldier, an artist, an athlete, or a laborer. I will be in your mutual relationship with the other person, even if you have no religious or ethnic preference. When you respect and embrace someone else, never jeopardizing or excluding anyone, you will find the path to truth, justice, love, fulfillment, honor, and power.

When you pray knowing that your prayer is not the one exclusive form I have chosen to hear, then I will listen to that prayer. Pray in any language, call my name whenever you feel you can and want to. Call me knowing that you are one with everything around you, and that you are also different. Call me knowing that I will help you and not hurt you. Meditate on me without arrogance or ego. Pray humbly, knowing your position is no higher or better than others. Pray that way and your prayer will be answered, your meditation will be complete. That is my way. That is your way. Adopt it and the purpose of your existence will be fulfilled.

From Mental Cripples to Creative, Spiritual Beings

I don't have much to do lately. I have a van. I transport people to various places but there have been no requests for transport in the last few days. It is a worrisome situation, because when I have less work, I can barely pay my bank loans. Payment on my communal service bill is long overdue. I fear that the small amount I have in the bank is not enough to cover all the debts that will be due in the fall when business slackens.

Therefore, you have to set priorities.

My priorities?

Organize your mind. Start by writing down an agenda or seasonal plan. You have to know exactly what you want, and then you can start implementing your plan. Everything starts with a thought. A thought is creative, the seed of the outcome.

But if you don't think through matters clearly, if your thoughts are vague, if you doubt your ideas can work, then the universal mechanism that supports your intentions will have no idea what to do. How can it implement an unformed plan? Even if you are more confused than you should be, you can always hope an opportunity will arise and note your priorities for when it does.

I repeat: Note down your plan. Then with an active prayer directed to me/you, start a cause-and-effect process to enact my intentions.

How can I do it? What active prayer are you talking about?

I will share with you one of the forms, but remember that there is more than one form. I never tend to uniformity, so the essence is the same whatever form it takes. Remember that. This can be your active prayer, or you can transform it into other forms, but its meaning will be the same. Listen carefully and know which button to press to fulfill your desires, plans, ideas, or ideals. This is a sensitive part of the book.

Focus and set your priorities. Take a notebook and write down items one by one. Write down what you want to achieve and what your goals are for the time being. I suggest you write down your goals explicitly, openly in this very book. Let your case serve as an example. This book will be a guide for those who sincerely search for truth inside themselves, and for all who search for the meaning of existence with an open heart. Set your priorities and we will describe active prayer that moves things forward and makes your intentions come true.

There is only one precondition for it: Under no condition should your desire be directed against anyone. Remember: UNDER NO CONDITION MAY YOUR DESIRE BE DIRECTED AGAINST SOMEONE. You don't curse, you actively pray. You don't spread hatred, but love. You don't seek revenge, but balanced energy. You sow good to enjoy a noble harvest.

And now … now I have to think and set priority desires and goals.

Yes.

And after that, I will discover that thanks to active prayer our wishes will be fulfilled.

Yes. Or in other words, active prayer helps you transform your thoughts into reality. A thought is creative. Remember how to think creatively again, how to act creatively and fulfill your own intentions creatively.

The next step develops on its own. You become creative, spiritual creatures. The process will conclude when you do. The circle will be complete and the meaning will be found. Mentally crippled people will turn into spiritual, creative creatures and pave the way toward me. Once you fully understand relativity, absoluteness will take on a new meaning.

Is this the way back to you? If it is, where are you? Where is your supreme residence? What awaits us there?

"Once you get back to me, you will never go back to a relative world." It is a promise which I gave in transcendental form to Krishna, to Arjuna at the battlefield of Kuruksetra. At the time of Leyletul'kadr I raised Muhammad to the sky where he discerned my shape at the throne of all visible and invisible worlds. Jesus saw me as Abba and entered the ocean of transcendental bliss. My worlds are endlessly diverse and unreachably mystical. My body is the source of that beauty. Everything that is created rests in my hands. I control every corner of my creation. All sounds reach my ear through an immensity of dimension. There is no way for me to fully describe in your language a single detail of the beauty I radiate. There is no way to put letters together and make a word or words that will be good enough to describe me.

What is the point of writing this book then? What is the point of our imagining you when we can't possibly imagine you? Why pray actively when we don't know who to address our prayers to or how to pray?

I would like you, as individual beings, to transfer yourselves from the state of mental disability into a spiritually creative state. That path toward me is paved with gold and emeralds. That is what you called a final path in your last book—a final path to me.

For that reason, you should actively pray. Some of your scholars have already recognized that form of prayer and called it scientific prayer. Whatever—call it active or scientific prayer—the main goal of that meditation is to reach intelligent creativity. Intelligent creativity will take you to spiritual creativity. Spiritual creativity will be the last door to open into my chambers. Come to me. "Some faces that day shall be Nadirah (shining and radiant). Looking at their Lord (Allah)."

Therefore, don't think that this process has no meaning. The fact that you can't see or understand me now does not

mean that you are not on the way to me. An active prayer will be the first step toward that destination. Set your priorities so that we can set them into motion and make them real. This applies to you as well as to all others reading this book.

Let's move!

Let's move, together!

Straight to the sky in an active prayer ...

Priority Desires and Active Prayer

Prioritizing my desires is not as easy as it sounds.

I am not a golden fish that will limit the number of your desires only to three. Liberate your visions, indulge in fantasies. Don't cramp yourself. Many of your desires are hidden in a reactive mind. Sort out as many you have one by one. Every one is purposeful. They will bring out no evil, but they have the capacity to offer good to all. Let your bright, unburdened mind express the desires of your heart.

Well then. The first desires will relate exclusively to me. I am not sure, how to put it, how pure they will be, or how relevant they will be to my work. To express desires publicly, in front of all, is almost the same as going into the street naked. I don't know how prepared I am to present all my desires.

Who is asking you to present all your desires? There is no need to feel embarrassed because of me, as I know every single desire you may have had, that you still have, and all you will have in the future. Don't let me stop you.

I don't know how listing my desires will affect other people. This is much harder to do than I initially thought it would be. I would like to classify desires. I think it will be better to express some and not others.

Do it the way you like it. Many people like and appreciate honesty. Confessing that you will not mention every desire

shows that you are honest. I too have my most intimate desires. Remember that everything starts from me, and so do relationships, desires, or emotions that you define as discrete. Discretion guaranteed.

I suppose that readers will start noting their priority desires at the same time. Let's start then:

1. First I would like to have physical, mental, and spiritual health for myself and people close to me, the ones I feel specially attached to. Health, I am sure, is inevitably important to functioning in life generally.

2. I would like to engage in some philosophical, artistic, and spiritual work that is fulfilling in a special way, and which will benefit me and other people who will follow that work one way or another.

3. I would like to profit from that work—and not just a little or to only a limited extent. I would actually like to make quite a lot of money from it and thus put an end to my fear, despair, and depression, which are caused by chronic lack of money.

4. I would like to equally divide the financial surplus. Between 10 and 20 percent of it, I would spend on humanitarian or charitable purposes. I would definitely do that.

5. Yesterday I moved my computer from my home in town to my weekend house in the country (a central Herzegovina village between Mostar and Stolac, behind the Kvanj hill). Since then I have been working on my book, *God Is a Woman*, out there. I have succumbed to a typical country idyll, which is good for meditative writing. Wind swings grapes on an old grape vine. Clouds sail along in the sky. August Sun, neither too strong nor too weak, shines over the horizon where the hills are continuous. It is difficult to say where one ends and the next one begins. Massive blue limestone giants cover the far end of the valley. There I feel as though time stops and I stop with it. Time and I don't go anywhere, like two primeval Bogumil tombstones[17] sank into dark clay and dry fern. Somewhere behind the last hilltop over

17   The name for monumental medieval tombstones that lie scattered across Bosnia and Herzegovina.

the horizon, the waves of the Adriatic break. Knowing there is the sea, almost within reach, keeps me in a slight ecstasy, feeling I am in the middle of what nature offers. I am in a privileged dimension from which I can peacefully and freely speak to my God.

6. Therefore, right here at this place, when the time for it comes, I would like to experience the complete realization of myself as a spiritual, creative being and thus surpass my own reactive mind, which I am having a hard time with.

I am on the second floor of our family house in the Rotimlja village enjoying that wonderful view. There is an upper terrace from this room, and a paved yard under the terrace. Behind the yard on the left, there's a dilapidated house with no roof, doors, windows, but with a corner porch, badly neglected, overgrown by a smelly plant called tree of heaven and tough weeds. Next to the old house, there is a garden that looks even more neglected than the house itself. A wild fig tree dominates the center of the garden and rises above thorn bushes and weeds all out of scale. In August, fig trees are full of sweet and delicious fruit. This wild tree, on the other hand, has not a single tiny fig. It looks like a collection of left-, right-, up- and down-springing bare twigs. Further on, there is an abandoned stable. Right behind that is a small, uncultivated field not larger than one thousand square kilometers.

I am gazing at that house, that garden, stable, and small field.

When I make money from selling the book and start planning further investments and works, I will have the following priorities: renovating the old house, cultivating the garden, constructing a swimming pool, turning the stable into a small summer house, and starting a garden in the little field. The house will be rebuilt in a traditional style. It will have the old Turkish residential architectural style with an oriental style sofa, corner porches, vaulted windows, filigree iron railings, a living room in the attic, and stone fireplace in the front of the room, a spacious bathroom, terraces, guest rooms, studies, rest and meditation areas, and bedrooms.

Here it is, one more desire of mine. To establish on the Rotimlja plateau my own spiritual awakening center, where people will socialize, work, grow healthy food, and gather from all over the world to share with me a vision for raising humanity higher toward fulfillment of each one's own existence in the universe, to share a vision and work on its coming true.

7. Worship your own God/Goddess with your body, mind, and spirit. To feel clearly, to experience and know that God worships me. To find the purpose of existence and sail toward the high seas of transcendental pleasure, to disappear in its immensity, irreversibly sail over the cresting waves of bliss, over sharp rocks and cliffs, under dark clouds and lightning as it cuts the dense air and hits the wild waters of an encompassing existence. To sail in the encompassing roar of unleashed energies and natural exhibitions. To travel, to sail, to travel … To travel with a most wonderful Mohini by my side, to travel and to be aware that every path has its end anyhow.

Remember! Remember, my dear, that all your prayers have already been answered. Your every desire has already been fulfilled. Yes. The process is ongoing—the awakening process raised awareness.

You are in that part of that process, the time component before your wishes are fulfilled. Without this part, how could you experience the fulfillment of a desire? That makes it a desire. The verb phrase *to wish* implies coping with the delay. What stands ahead is present and verbs such as *have* or *take*. You have the right to take or to have everything you want. A desire creates a thought about possessing or taking that object of desire. A thought is creative. Once you thank the universe for the realization of what you currently don't have, a thought about something outgrows the wish phase and leads to possession. In order for a thought to be creative, it has to be preceded by determined work on fulfilling the wish. Thoughts that do not include careful plans and work are unproductive thoughts or empty daydreaming.

DESIRE + PREVIOUS GRATEFULNESS TO THE UNIVERSE/ME FOR THE FULFILLMENT OF A DESIRE

+ A THOUGHT ABOUT HOW TO REALIZE THE OBJECT OF A DESIRE

+ TAKING UP SOME ACTIVITIES FOR THE PURPOSE

OF FULFILLMENT OF A DESIRE

= FULFILLMENT OF A WISH

= TO HAVE/TAKE THE OBJECT OF A WISH

The active prayer is the second step toward wish fulfillment. It includes and manages all phases up to the moment when the wish is fulfilled. Active prayer is advance gratefulness to me as I have already done all it takes to fulfill your wish. Once you master this sublime technique you will turn from mental cripple into smart creative being. And that is something already. That's a position which opens new vistas and makes distant expanses clear. That will be the first viaduct intersected toward the final path. Fast track. Bridges among star nebula. You will become masters. And no one will ever sing to you again: "Why did you take the bad way when you could have taken a highway …"[18]

I see. I think I do. But can I thank you in advance for something I don't have? How can I get this faith that everything will be the way I thought it would, the way I want it to be?

Well, in such a way that you will not believe in it.

I don't understand. How can you not believe in what you want, and still expect it to come true?

No. You will not believe it, you will KNOW it instead. You will know that I am here for you and that you exist and work for me and yourself. Check the first part of the book where we put knowledge against faith and hope ahead of it. Faith precedes knowledge, the absolute knowledge that something will happen or come to life. When you pray actively then that prayer is not based on faith that things will happen but on certain knowledge that things have already been realized. Most of you believe I exist or don't exist and that I will or won't answer certain prayers. A great step forward in <u>**achieving spiritual**</u> **mastery is the knowledge that an object**

18   Βοσνιαν–Ηερζεγοϖινιαν ροχκ ανδ ρολλ βανδ Zoster, On a rock I sit alone.

of desire has been achieved. What comes next is waiting for the implementation process, which is potent yet fragmentary. Then the object that was unfulfilled is fulfilled.

Uhg! It is not so easy as it may seem at first. It is not easy to disregard faith and replace it with knowledge about something.

Practice. Experiment. Practice to know and not merely to hope. When you hope for something, it may or may not come true. Activate your brain and train your mind to know.

To start with, you may believe. At least believe in what you know and then, with the passage of time, transform belief into a full and comprehensive knowledge. Let it be the first time. Let that be the way to do it. Practice satisfying your desires, from the simplest to the more complex and demanding ones. The technique is always the same. If you know how to build a house, you may also know how to build a skyscraper.

As a matter of fact, all of you have already mastered the applied knowledge technique, but at the primitive level of desire satisfaction. When you go shopping or walking in nature, you already know enough to make your intentions come true. Now, I am asking you a question: If you know you can start and finish your favorite walk outside before you go to sleep, why wouldn't you replace that form of knowledge to higher levels of desire? If you add to your knowledge your gratefulness to me for having satisfied your desire in advance, even if it has not come true yet in the constant present, then you are on the way to becoming masters. But many of you crumple because you haven't clearly defined a list of desires. You are confused since you don't know what you really want to do with your life. Your perspectives are narrow; there is no space. Perspectives are even darker if you have lost faith in my existence. You are not even sure that you yourself exist. Isn't it all a bad dream, unreal existence, a real absurdity? It would be better to give it up and become dust that we were created from.

But, no! You have neither been dust, nor can you ever be. You are life. An eternal life. You are magnificent, worthy, and fantastic. There is no woman, child, or man on this planet whom I am not whispering this message to. Now I am saying it publicly, in this book: You are alive! You are life! You are all worthy of everything when your values are based on love and general prosperity, when they are based on singlediversity, and not on segregations or distancing.

You are alive and fantastic. All secrets and mysteries are in you; you are on the path to understanding and discovering the new beings you are and will be. You are the light of the stars, the darkness of the night, and the blue of the summer sky. You are love, frenzy, passion, and cyclic existence. You have a right to everything, and you know that you have that right. Don't live to crawl, but to walk briskly and then to fly. It's time for you to take your life into your hands again and achieve the meaning of existence. You are not dust. You are not absurdity. It cannot be that you are not anything. You are Gods. Be what you are.

So help me God.

I Have Taken a Pill and Realized That I Don't Need God

Oh, how great it is to be talking to you. It's not that I approve of what you say—what's the point of approving of God? But this is so comforting, so meaningful. In your own unique way, you put things where they belong. You have seduced me with your brain and the knowledge you use to rule. Of course, you know everything, but maybe now I feel how much knowledge you are giving me. Now I am sure that something magnificent and sacred is happening while I am writing this manuscript, this future book. I know it for sure because when I read once again my words written at times of unique inspiration, I realize that I had no previous knowledge whatsoever about a number of topics that you explained. And then it is as though truth bursts out in my head and everything becomes crystal clear. I may not yet be sure I can apply the techniques you describe to my daily life, but I do understand the point of living and functioning better than before. I don't know what else to say. Thank you, thank you, thank you hundreds and thousands of times. I don't know what I did to deserve these great moments, but my gratitude reaches as far as the sky that you have raised high above us here on the Earth.

No need to thank me, even though I see your gratitude as a powerful way of satisfying your life desires. Don't analyze your desires. Don't analyze yourself either. As long as your decisions don't curtail other people's freedom and comfort, and as long as they are meaningful and purposeful, then follow my instructions and start making them come true. I have not created the world of good and bad people, capable

and incapable, more and less bright individuals. You are all equally capable and smart in the way and under the conditions that suit you best in that moment. There is no such person as one can be whatever he wants, but everyone can achieve a life that makes it possible for him to take a step forward. What would be the point of creating a life of hopelessness and suffering if such conditions became an end in themselves? Your world is not a valley of tears as many think. Your world is not the world of the dead or the poor. In the world where you live, you may realize the most sublime visions of what you want to be. This world is made for that purpose with you in it. Success is guaranteed, as long as I am the one putting a guarantee stamp on it. Do you really need any further proof?

No. No need for it. You are great. Every word of yours is a comfort; every encouragement of yours is so logical and complete that it puts even a cowardly, incapable person like me on firm footing. You pave the road out of a mental confusion. Of course, I haven't solved any of my problems yet, but for the first time I feel as if some of my problems can be solved and this can happen soon.

That's good. Never shrink from problems, regardless of how difficult they may be. Problems will come and go. They are inevitable in the cognizance phase where you are for now. But what's important for you is to learn how to deal with problems, understand them correctly, classify them, take a right stand, and then solve them.

There will be problems you will see as insurmountable. Don't make enormous efforts to surmount them. In such cases, always try to find life-saving mental peace, which, in a blink of an eye, can bring a thought that you can follow. Never make extraordinary efforts. Never fight against anything, whatever it is—humans, thoughts, or something else. Fighting is an action that results from lack of power. Express your power through your peace of mind, through a discrete contemplation. Don't quarrel or shout at others. Don't try to make your words louder than others. The true leader is the one who allows people to choose him to lead them. He is not the one who tries to impose his authority forcefully and without their consent.

Yes. Exactly. I agree. But then what happens when a problem, something I have managed to solve before, or that I'm not afraid of, comes back again? But this time it is much stronger and graver than before? I have had such an experience. Tell me how to behave in such an uncomfortable situation.

You are talking as though you are afraid of something.

Yes.

And you have overcome that fear?

Yes. I have even forgotten about this fear and its causes. For several years, four or five, I lived without certain fears that once gave me a hard time for months on end. And then I experienced the worst possible scenario. Those fears came back greater and more devastating than at any time before.

You are saying you have managed to overcome fear, but now it seems to have returned to you.

Yes. That's exactly what I am talking about.

Then you have not overcome that fear. Perhaps you have pushed it back, put it consciously or not into some part of you, thinking you have managed to overcome it for good. But that was not the case. If you ignore something, that doesn't mean it does not exist. The point is that up to now you have not managed to fully overcome that troubling fear.

I suppose you know what I am writing about. You know what "my fear" refers to.

Of course, I do.

I have neither the strength nor will to describe in detail what puts me in such a terrible position.

In fact, there is no need for you to write about your own experience. Anyway, I know very well all the facts about what you have experienced and what you will experience about that spot in your life line. On the other hand, there is no need to write about that event for the sake of other people, as everyone has his or her own fearful memories to suffer. All

of you have one thing in common: fear that you cannot get rid of, fear that blocks normal functioning, fear of everyone and everything, and fear of fear itself. **Now, it is time for you to learn more about fear, trouble, suffering, or mental illness.**

It sounds as if you are inviting people to group therapy.

Group or individual. People should understand it the way that suits them best. One thing is certain: Many need therapy right now. Mental therapy, if you prefer.

I think it's great to have God as a therapist. Can you say it is possible to have God for a therapist?

I don't see why it wouldn't be possible. I am your best friend, your best girlfriend, and eternal fellow-traveler. Not a single moment passes without my being with you through foul and fair. Being where you are in the process, you tend to forget that I am with you. But you can always notice that God is with you. It has always been thus and always will be as an inspiration and sublime message. As a clear thought and bright idea. As a path, guideline, and tool that will help you reach the other side. There is nothing that it is not me or that I cannot be.

It has always been and will be. So why wouldn't I be a personal therapist to each of you? Can you find a reason why I couldn't be?

I don't know. Perhaps because it is so difficult to believe such an idea.

But it is not only an idea. Why would I be giving up on you? To create you, give you freedom to act, and then give up on you for some reason? You can do nothing that will make me give up on you. Never have I given up on any of you, not for a moment. It is simply impossible. Get that possibility out of your mind. Simply push it out of your mind as an untruth and a destructive lie. And then you will start realizing that I am your eternal and unconditional friend.

This will lead to your understanding that I can be your inherent therapist, as well. Once you realize how it works between the two of us, you will grasp an essential truth about

our relationship. **You will become wise. Silent and wise. And when you are silent, wise, and aware I am with you at all times, your fear, anxiety, and uncertainty, bad thoughts, and destructive emotion will go away. Then you and I become one. As is the case now, so it will be in future.**

Yes. Very nice and comforting.

Isn't it the therapist's job to help you become peaceful and relaxed? Or more precisely, to help you liberate that healing condition from within?

Surely it is. You do it well. You are successful with me (at least from time to time, as there is still that problem), and I am sure other people will have the same experience.

All people—not only some, not only somewhere, and not only at some point of time. All people everywhere and at all times will have that experience. I promise. No one has ever been ignored for any reason. Therefore, stand up and understand that the mercy that I show you at all times is right under your nose and before your eyes. Take it and benefit from it. Benefit from your God. That is your only destiny. Everything else is a lie and mirage. Fear is the greatest mirage. Don't succumb to it …

How can one ignore fear? How can one overcome fear? How does one deal with it in an efficient way?

Forget about fight. Fight comes out of a lack of power. The time for fight ends when wisdom begins.

    Define first what exactly causes your fear. Consider all aspects of the condition and its source. And remember that there is nothing in the created world that can hurt you, kill or cripple you, nothing but your own thoughts about the way things are or might be.

    A bad thought is a stumbling block. A good thought heals. A bad thought is not purposeful. Such thoughts are based on untruths, lies, misconceptions, and prejudices. If you have bad thoughts for long, then, considering the fact that thoughts are creative, the bad will be active in your body, your life, and all that's around you. It will lead to depression, dysfunctional

existence, and diverse diseases. Nowadays that happens to many.

How can one avoid such an outcome?

By stopping bad thoughts.

Nevertheless, sometimes they overwhelm me. Sometimes it is impossible to make them go away. No matter how hard I try to change them, or replace them with better ones, they are simply too powerful to ignore. Despite my conscious efforts, they persist.

And it results in only one thing: Bad thoughts lead to chronic depression or anxiety over time.

Yes! Exactly. But can you change your thoughts when it seems impossible?

It is difficult to influence the brain's chemistry.

The brain's chemistry?!

Yes. I mean change in the same way you affect your blood quality, your liver, or your heartbeat. Why should I oppose anything that can be helpful for you? Why shouldn't it be I who sometimes writes your medical prescription? That is the role of science. Not to destroy lives, as is the case with the military industry, but to advance it, as the pharmaceutical industry should do.

You are suggesting that there is a pill to prevent bad thoughts?

There is no pill to prevent bad thoughts, but there are ones that stimulate the creation of certain hormones (serotonin) that are the chemical prerequisite for happiness and a good mood. Taking pills to promote mental recovery is an option, and it is not necessarily a fatal one as some may think. Especially now that medicine has advanced so much that it can identify and classify body parts and functions with which you exist. As long as you are with your body and around it, you neither must nor can ignore its existence and function. You have to look after your body in that way you somehow look after yourself while you are around it.

You mean that we are not in our bodies. We are around them.

The point is focus. You concentrate your energy and maintain your bodies to live with them. But you are not your body. It is only part of you as long as you exist on the level of matter. The soul creates and supplies the body with whatever it needs as long as the soul is with the body. When a soul releases the body, the body becomes matter—so-called lifeless matter. The dead body decomposes and disappears while the soul continues its life through time and space. That is why it is more correct to say that you are not in a body, but your body is in you.

You are superior to your body. As a result, you are responsible to it. If, under some circumstances, it stops producing certain hormones, then you should help it recover its natural function. You have to cure it.

The brain is a receiving organ, receiving input from your surroundings. It processes and sends out emotional energies related to particular objects, persons, experiences, and events. The brain is therefore a decision-making organ in every sense. When its function is seriously disturbed, you should help it. Although the reach of contemporary science has both positive and negative sides, use scientific achievements to improve the quality of life, and science will make sense for you.

So when in chronic depression, one should focus on pharmaceutical treatment.

In the narrow sense, yes.

And it will be enough to make me well, to transform bad thoughts into good ones.

The appropriate pharmaceutical treatment will reestablish hormonal balance in your brain. But it will not do much with what caused that hormonal imbalance. Together with pharmaceutical intervention goes psychological therapy, or in other words, spiritual therapy.

Spiritual therapy? What is spiritual therapy? Does that include resorting to certain prayers, mantras, or religious rituals?

No. It does not necessarily have to be like that—but it can

be. It's a completely personal decision. **Spiritual treatment can start with a simple thought such as: I am eternal, God is eternal, and I am with God. God is with me. Or some other thought which reflects your spiritual existence and accompanying powers. Spiritual therapy can go a step further and remind you that you don't need anything, including me, at the time of healing.**

At the time of healing we need neither you nor God!? I don't understand it. Such a claim sounds completely illogical to me. First, you convinced me that it is good to treat mental problems with pills and now you are telling me that in the same case we don't need anything, not even you.

I was not talking about care in the same case. I was talking about diverse levels of spiritual treatment and different ways to apply spiritual knowledge.

At a very low level of spiritual consciousness, as applies to most of you with whom I am communicating through this book, your body, senses, and mind have a more visible existence than your spirit, which is the essence of your existence. At times when your senses, body, and mind are the backbone of your existence and your acting, then it is natural that you are not aware of your spiritual powers. Some people are not even aware of the existence of themselves as spiritual beings. They don't believe in a spiritual dimension of life but only in a material one, the touchable one. Of course, in such a state of consciousness, every injury—bodily or emotional—excludes the possibility of spiritual mediation or spiritual treatment of the injury or the injured.

Simply put, you are oblivious of your spiritual superiority. If you are not aware of it, it does not mean you are condemned in any way. Your being unaware of the spiritual aspect is part of the process that will take you to complete and absolute awareness of it—no matter how painful it may seem to you. Therefore, curing a body is possible on the physical level. Otherwise, how would your wounds and your fractured bones heal, by themselves and with no one's mediation?

Why shouldn't you be able to heal, as well, emotional wounds including those that are large and significant—

at least in your eyes? However, using spiritual methods of healing, you will not keep the problem secret or delay its resolution. You will deal with it comprehensively and then all of a sudden you will realize it never existed, that there never were problems in your life or in the lives of people around you. The spiritual approach to life's problems makes them automatically disappear just as much as a wound starts healing when you cut yourself while shaving. The spiritual approach to problems removes them as obstacles. They become stepping-stones to further understanding of what you really are and always have been, even though you have forgotten it temporarily. Spiritual treatment will open your eyes even more, and you will understand that you were created in the image and likeness of God, that you are Gods yourselves.

What do I need so I can enjoy my existence? Nothing! Neither I nor you need anything. You are created in the image and likeness of me. You are me, I am you, and still we are different. We are Singlediverse.

Therefore, travel and see the world around you. Travel and understand yourself in that world where you live. Don't miss a single opportunity, because the first time you have an opportunity, you will surely benefit from it as you benefit from me. And once you have benefited from me, you will realize that you have never needed me. Once you realize that you have never needed me and won't need me in the future, you will open your arms and embrace me. You will do it the same way as a child who embraces his mother before he falls asleep after suckling.

"Your body is a fairy tale, your arms are mother, that's how I see you …"[19]

Fantasy …

---

19   Song "Fantasy" from Branimir Štulić.

Don't Count Your Chickens before They Are Hatched, and Change the World

I live in Bosnia and Herzegovina. It is unbelievable how life keeps showing us how it is difficult, even impossible, to create a state that will suit the diverse people living there.

For those less informed, I would like to point out that Bosniak-Muslims, Serbs-Orthodox, and Croats-Catholics live in Bosnia and Herzegovina. There are other minorities here too, but these three ethnic groups are dominant and constituent.

From 1992 through 1995 a war raged in Bosnia and Herzegovina. Some try to call it a civil war, while others call it aggression by at least one, or not more than two, neighboring countries. The violence was successfully ended by the Dayton Peace Accords (DPA), which the three conflicting sides signed in March 1995 in Dayton, Ohio, USA. Even though many positive things have been done in postwar Bosnia and Herzegovina, primarily thanks to the international community acting through the OHR and OSCE,[20] I still can't help thinking that the deep distrust and intolerance of our long history lives on. It is as though war is a fatal destiny for us and our country. We have never had forty or fifty years without shooting, without warring sides rising

---

20   Office of the High Representative and Organization for Security and Co-operation in Europe.

against each other. Everyone considers others responsible for this. Certainly, there were innocent victims on all three sides. Nevertheless, no one can deny that Bosniak Muslims suffered the greatest death toll in the last war. The numbers are not settled, but with sound reason it is estimated that from 1992 through 1995, 60,000 to 80,000 Bosniak civilians were killed here.

In the twelve years since the DPA was signed, the gaps among these national groups has not been bridged. For me, Bosnia and Herzegovina is a living European and world political problem. What position is one to take with regard to it? Is it possible to do anything to move affairs in the right direction?

Today, more than ever, Bosnia and Herzegovina has a historical opportunity to set standards of international agreements and political compromises that will serve as an example to the entire world. You can always take things in your hands and rule your own destinies more positively than before. Of course, you may continue abandoning yourselves to empty ethnic and religious raptures and thus create a hellish environment that you can hardly manage to get out of. As for Bosnia and Herzegovina, its key problem is not nationalism.

What is the problem then if it is not nationalism?

The country's overall development is interrupted by the common citizens' low spiritual consciousness, regardless of their ethnic background. Their general ignorance, the insufficient, even malevolent education they receive— these have tormented Bosnia and Herzegovina from times immemorial. From 1992 to 1995 human stupidity climaxed. At the time, whole brigades of people sought only to torture and exterminate others from different ethnic backgrounds. They were victimized regardless of their gender, age, or utter noninvolvement in the war. Thus, concentration camps were filled. A great number of people were brutally killed and then buried in mass graves in secret places. These mass graves are now being discovered one after another, and they point to the inhuman character of crimes that took place there.

Why don't you point out that Serb criminals led the killing

ahead of all others? In Mostar, Croatian criminals established concentration camps for many Bosniak and Serb civilians. Horrible Islamic terrorism also caused a tremendous loss of life. Islamic terrorists "imported" from some Arabic countries, together with certain local people who joined them, terrorized innocent Serb and Croatian civilians and captured soldiers. But, judging by the scope and the level of brutality, crimes against Bosniaks in Bosnia and Herzegovina were the most intense.

Should one remain silent at that? Is it good to remain silent for the purpose of achieving a quick, surface reconciliation?

Try not to point your finger at each other. You should rather cooperate toward raising spiritual awareness. It is not that one should remain silent when it comes to the truth about crimes, and it is not that I am deliberately skipping facts related to those crimes. I'd point out, rather, that if you first determine the state of mind that turned some people into predators, you will do more to resolve inter-ethnic problems.

On one hand, you can't accuse others—transferring the burden of guilt to entire ethnic groups—and turn a blind eye toward crimes that happened in your name as a member of a particular ethnic group.

What would one do then? I am not clear. What position could one take toward the horrors of the recent war so that no one feels deprived and hurt?

Everyone will start by putting their own house in order.

Mostar Muslims would have much more right to resolve past grievances in concentration camps such as Heliodrom, Colleges, or Soko, if they confessed before everyone that Bosniaks also committed crimes against Croats in Grabovica and Trusina. Also, Bosniaks would more quickly resolve the issue of murders in Srebrenica, if they condemned crimes against those Serb civilians who remained in Sarajevo during the siege.

But it is about a number. It is impossible to put an equal sign between the number of Bosniaks killed in Srebrenica (8,300 killed in five days) and the number of Serb victims in Sarajevo (1,000 killed in five years). These crimes are not equal in scope and suffering.

Can you equate one crime as equally serious with another? Less awful? More? I am asking you as a Muslim, whose rights are jeopardized in Bosnia and Herzegovina.

Of course I can. It is not the same when the number of victims in one case reaches thousands and in the other, dozens, maybe hundreds. Obviously, on one side it was highly organized violence, while on the other, one cites sporadic cases and incidents.

Then remember a verse from the Quran: "If anyone slew an innocent person it would be as if he slew the whole mankind and if anyone saved a life it would be as if he saved the life of all mankind ..."

I am not mentioning this verse to refute you by quoting from your own Holy book, since my aim is never to refute other people's positions at any time or place. It is my intention to have you come to certain conclusions that will broaden your horizons and help you get unstuck from prejudice. To be static is not good; sometimes it is even dangerous. Therefore, raise your eyes and decide if you can still make a step forward in the surrounding darkness.

So, what is your message to Serb authorities in the Republika Srpska and Croats and Bosniaks in the Federation?

Hold open trials to process all and any crimes done in the name of an ethnic group. Don't hesitate even for monstrous characters and massive crimes. Process all relevant evidence and statements. Call all the victims who are willing to testify and let them speak freely in your courts with no fear of revenge. Let a Serb judge and jury pass the verdict on a Serb criminal, let a Bosniak pass the verdict on a Bosniak, and Croat on a Croat. Then, let representatives of all three ethnic groups jointly reach a conclusion and commit their groups to this: Henceforth, no ethnic group or authority will allow a single ethnic crime to go unpunished.

You all be the advocates of such a declaration. Thus, you will be on the path to closing a bloody page in your country's history. You will be on the path to new prosperous ideas that will propel you to unimagined limits of inter-ethnic human

achievement. And that is my message.

It sounds good, almost utopian, I admit. I don't think, however, that RS[21] authorities are willing to prosecute criminals from their own side.

Not for the time being. Neither Bosniak nor Croatian political representatives are willing to, either. For now, you are stuck in one place. Your spiritual perception is low. You have a highly developed ethnic and religious conscience, but it is obvious that ethnic and religious affiliation don't take you far in terms of personal development, as an individual or a society.

Why is it so?

It is because your essence is not ethnically or religiously determined. Those are all fabrications resulting from historic, social, and natural circumstances. You constructed them artificially in your minds by making decisions that led to stagnation, conflict, and disagreement.

But it is not necessary to give up ethnicity or religion in order to move on. It is not necessary to obliterate ethnicity in order to create an ethnically neutral society. I am saying it isn't necessary, it isn't even undesirable. The same applies to religion and everything else. It is not wise to prohibit, block, or destroy anything at any time or for any reason. Sometimes, the end does not justify the means, as means determines the nature of an end. Therefore, everyone should experience his or her own phantom-like identities, as otherwise, they will not understand that they are only phantoms.

Interesting way of thinking. And how can someone tell Ivo Mijo Jović, Haris Silajdžić, or Milorad Dodik that their way of thinking is phantom-like, then expect them to change their thinking and then change reality on the ground?

You will not say a word to anyone. Go back to my previous comment. Everyone has to live their own illusions in order to understand the futility of those illusions.

---

21 Republic of Srpska. An entity in the new post-war organization of Bosnia and Herzegovina from which a huge number of non-
Serbs were expelled or killed during the last war.

I don't understand it again. How can we resolve an impasse when the very people deciding our country's secular arrangement live their own illusions and have neither the strength nor will to move things in a positive direction?

I have spoken about it. No one is powerful enough to make people change, but one can indirectly encourage people to grow personally. Your Singlediverse nature determines this, too. Your unconditional freedom determines it as much as it prompts people's mutual dependence. You can't directly change the way today's politicians think, but you may and should focus on changing your own self.

When you change for the better and take a fresh perspective on people and things, you will set an example for others to initiate their own spiritual and creative change. Each of you finds his own way of inherent awakening. At the same time, each of you is and will remain unique.

This learning was great, inspirational, but what is it supposed to mean in our everyday routine? What is it supposed to mean to Bosnia and Herzegovina and the world, after all?

Your world rests upon you. Her world rests upon her. His world rests upon him. You are creators of your own worlds. There is not only one world. Each of you has his or her own. Each of you can influence your own world. And that is the essence of a world change. You can't go out in the street now and spread word that a new world is opening before you. You can't appear on a TV or radio program and single out politicians you think live in the illusion of their own mental prejudices. As a matter of fact, you can do it (nowadays many politicians and intellectuals are singled out in different media), but the outcome of such publicity would not get you far; it would be counterproductive.

Therefore, your literary and meditative work is the best way to encourage people to start changing their own worlds, attitudes, orientation, and ways of thinking.

It is the way to change the world: Create critical mass by depending on each other. Then, through a sequence of events, you will organize yourselves into an association of creative individuals at your local level. The number and

diversity of people who join will grow gradually. They will start organizing themselves at a global level. Your world is not a global village—your world is a global, interactive world of endless possibilities. Use them and overcome the terrible states of distrust, exclusiveness, and intolerance embodied by all state, national, or religious systems.

Oh! I see it now. I hope that many readers will recognize the capacity and significance of what has just been said. You are an amazing interlocutor—patient, tactful, and influential. I don't know what to say. I will perhaps open an e-mail account when I reach the end of the book so that readers everywhere can present their ideas, impressions, and proposals. I am changing my world. Everyone should start changing their respective worlds, since our worlds obviously need comprehensive changes.

You have got it. Many have understood it now. All those who have decided to separate truth from untruth are now on the way to regaining awareness. The idea of communicating with others by e-mail is good, and I support it. That could be the first way of organizing that was inspired by this book. Once you establish a spiritual-creative base, you will recognize all other similar organizations that you share goals with, and they will recognize you, too. Critical mass will be achieved. Many people make the place where you live, and where your descendants will live, into a center of spiritual and creative advancement, of material plenty, a place of cognizance and self-confirmation. It can be a world of united, unique, and diverse people—in short, the world as it is meant to be. Change others in such a way that you will change yourself, and let others change you in such a way that they change themselves first.

Don't condemn. Value one another mutually and individually. Everyone can be both judge and jury for himself. Not to pass a judgment that drowns him in the sludge of guilt, but to identify his inner self. Let him find what he is not and has never been. And so, with a new understanding of something in his inner self that is not typical of him, every man opens the door to his own freedom.

There Is One Sun, the Same Air, and the Same Water Everywhere

Therefore, it is possible to have associations at the local and global level which can affect the changes so much needed by this world?

Of course it is possible. Not only that it is possible but also much needed. A new Singlediverse association in the form of a New World Association would not base its work on the power of a mass, or the power of more or less secret political and economic lobbies as is the case with all political organizations which have existed at the global level. It is rather synchronized work of self-reliant individuals from all over the world regardless of their ethnicity, religion, or race. The efficiency of that organization would not be based on number of members but on their awareness.

How can you know if a person is aware enough or not? Which psychological features should possible members of that association have?

It is impossible to determine any criteria, at least not the way you imagine them. You don't have to have a higher formal education to be considered as acceptable to such a society. This society should not be *secret*. Further, if a person does not have a formal education, it would not necessarily mean that he does not have his Singlediverse consciousness well developed which put him into a group of individuals with more developed awareness. What does it mean to be aware? Nothing, but to be honest. To be objective and calm. If a

person acts as in an honest, calm, and objective manner, then he acts in his best interests. Today, in your world, people tend to think wrongly that to achieve one's goal means to curtail interest of other persons in any way. But it is simply not correct. The world affairs nowadays, as well as the very well-known historical facts, prove it wrong. It is impossible to achieve your own goals and at the same time to deprive other people of their rights and interests. You can't be an exploiter, tyrant, parasite, executor, or dictator and expect to be acting in your best interests. Anyway, you may be thinking that you, by violating other people's rights, achieve your own goals and the goals of people around you, but time will show you were wrong. It is so strange how little you have learned from your own history, the very recent one. Therefore, the features the future New World Association members are expected to have, should be based on an individual's honesty, calmness, and objectivity.

What does it really mean to be honest, calm, or objective? Does it mean that, by not depriving others of their rights we are not working against our best interests? How it is possible to provide ourselves and at the same time, to provide other people around us? Aren't goods scarce? Aren't the world resources limited? After all, wars are waged for that reason.

The illusion of insufficiency. For thousands of years humans have been suffering from a chronic illusion of insufficiency. To have that illusion means to deprive one of the endless goods that belong to him. If you live and act thinking that you don't have enough goods you need to survive in the world you live in, then you will either go through an agony because of that way of thinking or you will take away from others everything you believe you need to survive. You would establish violent relations among people, the relations between victims and predators, slaves and slave owners, capitalists and workers, aristocracy and serfdom. Your entire history is full of revolutions, wars, uprisings, and rebellions by the exploited against exploiters. After such violent historical happenings, those formerly exploited turned exploiters. Wars have never been waged and revolutions conducted to establish more fair human relations, but in order for the oppressed to become oppressors. And so is the case today. A number of people believe that this is the only way to see your future. However, technological advancement has made unseen changes to the planet. Mass destruction weaponry you have at your disposal makes any future war at the global level equally dangerous for all. It is, by all means, true that there are no good or bad nations or religious groups. All current ethnic groups and surely all religious groups live fully their illusion of insufficiency. In the world where the illusion of insufficiency is so obvious, changes are necessary. But not to produce more weaponry and create more sophisticated weapons of mass destruction. Force and terror will never provide you with safety and personal interest satisfaction. Resorting to force and terror simply goes against two fundamental rules of living in the universe, including your planet. Don't make the same mistakes over and over again. Be aware that there is enough of everything around you that you need to continue your life and preserve species. Not only for six billion living people, but also for all that will be born in the near and distant future. Dozens of billions of people will be able to share this space and with the fair distribution of wealth, each of them can become rich or a millionaire, as you like to say. It is true, indeed. It is not about the amount of resources. It is about the narrowed mind of an individual who lacks a proper perception of the world around him. Therefore, take the illusion of insufficiency away from your own lives and make it up with honesty, objectivity, and calmness. You will see that the world in which you live has become a better and nicer place to live at.

If there is enough of everything on our planet then why are there people dying of hunger, why is there a lack of oil in the world; does it mean that we can be endlessly cutting tropical forests and dig out ore as there will always be enough of them for everyone and everything?

To distribute resources correctly and to use them rationally does not mean to utilize energy and natural resources without any plan or purpose. When I say there is an abundance of supplies for everyone, it does not necessarily mean you can burn the planet and expect it to renew straight away. To manage resources in an appropriate manner and rationally means to pay more attention to investments and research related to renewable sources of energy than to those that are limited. In such way, you may use solar, water, or wind energy more than you do when it comes to energy we get from ore, gas, or oil. If only 20 percent of the money invested in your military industries had been invested into research and developing solar energy sources, we would have had a permanently resolved issue of energy resources for all and at all locations. Most of the reasons for waging wars would cease to exist. At least 60 percent of the money you are investing into military could be used to achieve a more efficient and natural food production system and to develop clean technologies. Solar, water, or wind energy would be produced in an environmentally friendly manner and you would not be faced with climate change consequences such as hurricanes, typhoons, floods, volcanoes, earthquakes, etc., or the greenhouse effect. To use renewable resources of energy means to save nonrenewable energy resources, to create a huge surplus of money and capital, which could then be used to systematically resolve problems all over the world such as poverty, unemployment, a lack of education, and health care. If we would start today a healthy reform of national and global organization and overall acting on this planet, in no more than ten years we will be able to see positive results. A very bad place to live would become a place where unique and happy people live.

It's unbelievable that many haven't got it yet. It's unbelievable that the key political, economic, military, or religious activity organizers in the entire world are the people without clear and proper vision of the future of the world and every single nation there.

Most probably, they still don't have a counterpart in terms of different political and social organization. Especially because of the fact that these can be the last moments before mass destruction of what you call contemporary civilization.

Well, it seems that we are really on the edge of a catastrophe, a nuclear and chemical war that would pose a complete destruction of all contemporary values.

Even though I am able to see everything that is going to happen in the future and that I know perfectly well the past and all current conditions, I have never jumped to conclusions, nor will I do it in the future. You will never hear from God about your future. Nothing precise. I have only pointed out that a catastrophe may happen on your planet, but it does not have to be. Your matrix of comprehensive conscience will be deciding about it. I recommend your acting on it in a timely manner and in a good faith. The decision is all yours. Just as much as it could be your decision to plead for a New World Association. It is time for people who think differently to express their positions. Despite many shortcomings, there is at least one significant achievement of contemporary civilization.

Is there?

Of course, there is. And that is the moment you can use. Freedom of choice of authorities and democracy are not such a farce as some would like to present it. After all, current world affairs reflect the matrix of contemporary conscience you all create together. You have the power to create new political associations and, thanks to your votes, you have the power to give them a new meaning on the contemporary political scene.

Have there already been such political parties or they are still to be established?

Some of the political parties seem to have already been aware of the dead-end street that mankind is heading to. They plead for a change of course. Obviously, their voice is not strong enough to be heard at the world political scene. I don't want this book to become a political and propaganda pamphlet. Therefore, I am not going to mention the names of these parties or their leaders. I am not going to mention the names of parties from any part of the world which are still in power and in thrall to outdated conservative political forms. Find out by yourself who is who at the world political scene. Use your own logic and fairness and you will get a clearer picture. Lies, destruction, and conspiracy have been dominating global political and economic courses. However, quite many well-intentioned people from all over the world have still been indecisive regarding numerous political options that are available. A new political initiative needs to focus on that group of people that are still indecisive despite the most powerful political forces on the scene. You would be quite surprised to learn how many they are and how eager they are to jointly make the first, significant move toward getting out of the life of madness in which they got into. And they are not only black, white, yellow, or red. These are not only members of Orthodox, Catholic, Hindu, Muslim, Jewish, Protestant, or Buddhist religion. These are not only men or women. Only workers, peasants, landowners, or capitalists. Nobody from only one or only some out of all existing groups. Many people, regardless of which geographic area they come from, their ethnic or religious affiliation, and race strive toward Singlediverse association and perhaps it is the right time now to focus on such an initiative.

> My Sun warms you all,
> My water feeds you—everyone without exception.
>
> You all breathe the same air,
> Above all of you is the same firmament.
>
> I am the God of you all,
> You are all part of Me,
> I am in the heart of everyone—without exception.
>
> We are Singlediversity.
> Single and Diversity.
>
> My will be your will,
> your will be my will,
> And the purpose of each and everything will be fulfilled.

So be it. My dear, let it be so.

Is God Spineless?

How can one establish hierarchy in such a society?

Easily. Humans are quite experienced, and they have significant knowledge of social organizing. But whenever a hierarchy of authority becomes an end in itself, a problem will arise. You shouldn't fall into that trap. Do not establish a hierarchy that can suppress freedoms to protect the comfort and position of people at the top of the social structure.

The point should be to establish a functional, mass society that makes caring for the individual its priority. Create a society focused on the individual and not one that requires the individual to focus on society, as has been the case many times. A group of self-confident, satisfied individuals represents the backbone of a successful society.

In all up-to-date forms of social grouping—socialism, communism, capitalism, feudalism, slaveholding, monarchy— the individual is subordinated to society, and as a result, he is the victim of society. Today, because you recognize money's kingship, you are witnessing a social order ruled by the economic elite. In other words, capitalists and liberals have given money artificial control over people and goods. They have concentrated that power in international institutions, thanks to which they control the whole world.

Are you talking about the International Monetary Fund and the World Bank?

You decide who I am talking about. Everyone should decide who I am talking about. I am not doing this for propaganda purposes. God is not an activist or opponent of any state apparatus or organization in the world.

It seems so …

Say it. Say what you think.

I don't feel comfortable and it seems inappropriate.

Say it anyway. You can't make me feel uncomfortable or hurt me. It would be good to say what you think.

Well. Anyway, I can't find a more appropriate term. To have a neutral position about everything that is going on in the world and not to point toward what causes problems … it indicates … weakness of character.

And now what? Will you be hit by a bolt of lightning? Will you be chased by thunder? Will you have a stroke?

I don't know, but you do.

I know it already, and you know it, too. Or more precisely, you *want to* know what will happen to you if you publicly call God spineless.

I really don't know what will happen to me. Currently, things couldn't be worse than they are.

Well, then, what would you do to me if I called you a spineless fool?

I do something to you?! I think I couldn't do anything against you. I don't have that power.

Let's assume you do.

You think … I should assume I am God and you are me.

It's an interesting assumption, even though I and you—we are One in the end. Anyway, for the purpose of our having a comprehensive debate, let's assume that I tell you, God, to your face that you are a fool and spineless. How would you treat me?

I might give you a light tap and then laugh uproariously. I

don't know. It would not be a good idea for me to become the Almighty. Have you seen Jim Carrey starring in *Bruce Almighty*?

I am a coauthor of all movies. So I know it is both a comic and educational movie. But, let's go back to the topic we started. I understand that you, as God, would treat me (not being God), with love and not with hatred and revenge, if I called you names in front of everyone.

Yes, it would definitely be from love.

What do you want to say publicly? That you would be a better God than I am?

Uh-oh!

Tell me if that's what you want to say?

No. Definitely not. You cunningly put me on thin ice. I give up. You always treat everyone with love. I agree. But in this exchange you have slyly disempowered me in a well-argued manner. Does it mean that you are sometimes cunning or astute?

Why wouldn't slyness sometimes be a tool of love? Any skill used to fulfill yourself or other people is a well-used skill, and that is all right.

Now, we have started several topics simultaneously. I have a few more questions I would like to ask you.

Go step by step, for better understanding.

Ok.

Question No. 1: How is it possible for God not to have clearly expressed positions about a particular problem?

Even if we accept as fact that we work with a *neutral* God, how is it possible, in good faith, to avoid misinterpretation of what you say?

You are saying that you are a coauthor of all movies. I suppose then that you are the coauthor of all art and cultural forms from times immemorial. However, I can't agree that all movies, songs, poems, or books are art. Where is the border between kitsch and high art? Doesn't God cross that border, if there is one?

We are moving in the right direction. Your questions are apt, and my answers will be relevant to the dilemmas that puzzle you.

I don't doubt that you will answer questions fully. What bothers me more is whether I will remain open to your unique dictation—and for how long. I am not concerned that you will make an error; my doubts and fears are about my own spiritual creativity.

Your doubt is both good and bad. When I use the words *good* and *bad* I mean being purposeful or nonpurposeful, useful or useless, progressive or reactionary. Consider those connotations, and then two words—good and bad—will take on a different, more purposeful meaning. Your self-doubt is good, a positive feature leading to growth. Be open up to more than internal criticism. You should responsively and openly take criticism from other people and institutions. When you correctly evaluate criticism, be it by yourself or from others, then your next steps will be more progressive than before. It's development. Criticism and self-criticism, properly directed and accepted, surely follow the path of general development and prosperity.

On the other hand, if criticism arises from blind self-doubt or is nonconstructive sniping by others, it will not have a positive effect on you and your work. Therefore, don't criticize only for the sake of criticizing. Criticize if you want to express a constructive opinion in good faith, when you consider that something could become better and bigger than it is. This refers especially to pieces of art that you consider less worthwhile.

Therefore, never doubt your being a spiritually creative creature. All of you really are spiritually creative creatures. Use your self-criticism and doubt to grow. There are no limits to your development. Your goal lies in the infinity of beauty that you are and in the infinity of beauty that I am. Your goal lies in the infinity of beauty of what we are.

I see. I think I do.

If you don't understand something completely, you may understand it the very next moment. You have trained yourself

153

very well. I find it easy to work with you.

Do you? Really?

Yes. True—as true as it is that each of you reading this text is capable of initiating your own dialogue with me. Remember that. Or at least believe you know it. Or at least believe that you will find it out soon. And I will start fluttering between lines as a healing truth and expanding knowledge. If not immediately, then, in a moment of inspiration and enlightenment. You are all spiritual, creative beings. This book is a clear call to use your endless abilities. You may use your spiritual creativity in any sphere of action, if the action is purposeful and progressive.

Is a dialogue with you possible only in a written form?

Of course not. I have said and I am repeating, "You may use your spiritual creativity in any sphere of action if the action is purposeful and progressive." And an action is purposeful and progressive if it is in line with our own interests. Your interest will be served when it does not violate the interests of others or, even better, when it aligns with the interests of all others as they are complementary and developing. That may be the key to forming new local and global organizations. I am talking about the New World Association. I am talking about purposeful Singlediversity.

Yes. We are going back to the issue of God's being neutral. Does your neutral position leave the door wide open to many diverse but opposing explanations of your thoughts?

I am not neutral. I simply don't want to oppose the two fundamental rules of living as that would undermine the pillars of purpose. The way it is now, it has been until now and will be in the future. When I talk about certain psychological phenomena in you as individuals, or about certain phenomena in your groups or societies, it is not my intention to point my finger at anyone or to accuse, call names, criticize destructively, or incite. That is not my goal. It is not my way.

I focus on helping each of you recognize in yourselves a feature that needs to be changed. And that does not mean being neutral. I am talking about your shortcomings, as

individuals, and what you create in your mutual relationships. I am clearly speaking about those matters. I am proposing solutions and pointing to them.

Your justice system has already demonstrated, repeatedly, that punishment doesn't stop crime. Consequences don't stop bad choices. One nail does not drive out another, after all, at least not without resistance. I am talking about development, not about punishment. I am talking about the process, and not revolution or war.

I am pointing to ideas and advising you. I have never given you an order, because my every order is inevitably carried out. I am not God of powerlessness, but God of power. It is impossible for me to decide something that fails to come true. To that end, I have decided to make you happy and creative beings. Use your freedom. Both the IMF president and the Islamist group leader plotting against globalized interests have the same right to freedom. I am not going to single out any of them or accuse anyone. But I am going to call everyone to take a second look at what they do.

If your thoughts and actions cause exclusion and torment, then constructively reexamine your intentions and their causes. Start acting in your own best interest, not in violating the rights and freedoms of others. Act for mutual relations and growth. The point of your life is not to destroy life. You cannot destroy life anyway, but you can deprive it of its meaning. And its meaning is to collaboratively overcome illusions of insufficiency and detachment. Only then will victory be complete. The victory of all, no one beat, no losers.

Do so and you will do it right.

Seriously and Frivolously

I am sorry to have said you are spineless.

Ha, ha, ha …! Ha, ha, ha … And I haven't even given you a gentle tap. A gentle, quick hit, as you would give me. Who is the better God then, me or you?

You are making fun of me.

And why shouldn't we be joking a bit? It is not good for this book to be too serious. I am not as solemn as many make me seem. If I were like that, I would have no choice but to let you create one pretty serious world. A dangerous and serious world. Are you enjoying it?

I personally am not. I have written somewhere something about being serious. I'll try to find it in a folder. Perhaps it will fit well into the continuation of the book.

I have found a text dubbed:

SERIOUSLY AND FRIVOLOUSLY

When people ask me what my job is, if I am a preacher or a writer, I always say: I'm a writer.

A preacher only preaches and a writer can be both.

In other words, when you preach as a writer, people don't have to take you seriously.

I believe that a key problem is how people take things too seriously. They talk seriously, they eat seriously and politely, they should be polite at work, serious in a relationship, serious while traveling, in bed, in negotiations, in an elevator, in the street, on the plane, on holidays, in war, at peace, while praying, driving, or toasting in the sauna.

Of course, many writers make their writing pretentious and serious, so people who are already too serious don't really want to read anything serious again.

We offer fun, satire, and fooling around. I think that God should not be serious at all. If God were serious, monkeys would not laugh and jump on each other's heads, picking lice from their scalps and eating them happily. If God were serious, there would never be such a great comic actor as Danilo Bata Stojković.

The best thing happens when you get something serious out of a frivolous situation. But even then, you don't have to take it *too* seriously. If you do, you will return heavily to your dull daily routine.

Some think it is enough merely to survive life. That grim business should be resisted. Aren't there too many forces dragging us down and threatening to trap us forever in darkness and oblivion? Seriousness is worse than murder. As a matter of fact, seriousness is one of the most heinous ways to kill yourself or people around you.

At the beginning of the 1920s most of the people from the western and central Balkans took politics so seriously that crime and a big war resulted. You know how it works, everyone was deprived of his or her rights and everyone wanted their own piece of land. Then they were unable to agree about to how to divide the land, water, and air, so true *murder* started.

They were all dead serious—army leaders, presidents, and soldiers. They translated their loathsome seriousness into a deadly plan and yet another crime against humanity took place in the Balkans.

Today, everyone takes his own political game very seriously. As a result, we are up to our necks in shit caused by cultural, religious, and racial rifts among the world's big nations.

We frivolously point to various serious things.

Curse, Hell, Love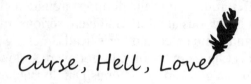

It's been a couple of days since you last sat at your computer.

True. Is that supposed to mean something?

Nothing special, except that you should reread the text "Seriously and Frivolously."

Why should I? You think that text is not good enough?

No. I have no right to make such an assessment. I'd rather say that some words there don't serve the purpose.

Are you referring to some inappropriate words?

That's right. Inappropriate word choice, in the context of what you properly said about *seriously* and *frivolously*, doesn't belong in the paragraphs you wrote.

Golly! You are not as liberal as I supposed you would be. You insist on morality the same way clergy and certain theologically conservative circles do. "There is no place for cursing! Please, behave yourselves!" I am disappointed. Is it common for people to be cruel in war, but not proper if I call war "shit?"

I am not saying it is not common. You can't say I approve of cruel behavior in a war. But the inappropriate word "shit" does not say what you meant to say.

In other words, you stick to moralizing. Once I used to like a line: "Block the passage to rotten moralists, block the passage to cuckolds, block the passage to Stalinists, block the passage to all."[22]*

I am not moralizing. I *am* saying that the word "shit" does not meet the meaning of what you wanted to say. As a matter of fact, I would like to ask you a question: Do you want to condemn a crime, or do you prefer to reexamine the psychological moment when a mind was inspired by criminal intent?

I think it would be more functional to work on a psychological profile of criminals.

Then, if you want to treat someone psychologically, inappropriate words will not be of much use. You can't be offensive and, at the same time, expect to encourage positive changes in yourself or society. Cursing usually signifies a lack of power, impotence. Haven't you noticed that cursing, offenses, and fights usually go hand in hand?

Yes. But it is not the same to curse and then kill as it is to curse because somebody has been killed.

Of course it's not the same. I am not equating different categories of behavior and speech. I am explaining powerlessness. In fact, by cursing and killing, a murderer confirms his spiritual immaturity and powerlessness to do anything purposeful about his circumstances. To curse about someone's behavior reveals powerlessness to influence or change the psychological factors that cause crime and hatred. Not only in the BiH war, but in wars throughout history, whether you have heard of them or not.

So what should be done, if it is not good to curse?

It is good to exert a positive influence on negative social conditions, but you can't achieve it by swearing or encouraging any form of hatred. Not even insisting on legal criminal procedures will promote critical changes in society. Don't condemn or evaluate yourself or others. You should rather focus on a positive change within yourselves. That is the way

---

22   Uradi nešto, Branimir Štulić.

to lead others toward change.

And what if it is impossible to change others? What if a criminal keeps insisting on justifying his crime, even when facing justice? At the International Court in the Hague, Netherlands, few people pleaded guilty of war crimes in the former Yugoslavia.

The case is complex. However, I believe that your contemporary legal system, too, has a quite negative impact on justice. Legal systems you have created within state or international institutions don't aim to get to the bottom of criminal intent and thus reveal the true cause of crime. These institutions simply sanction criminals as individuals. Each of the accused is fully aware and feels their guilt deeply in their hearts. But despite their introspection, they will never publicly plead guilty. Instead of following the voice of conscience, throughout the entire legal proceedings these people follow their self-preservation instinct. And that is no good for criminals or victims. It is not good for your country's future, in particular. Don't you see that episodes of bloody human history keep repeating?

Do you propose a comprehensive change in the legal system?

I propose you each conduct a comprehensive change of your own psychology, whether you are judges or suspects, criminals or victims, doctors or patients. Everyone from any ethnicity, race, or religion can do much to make life meaningful by working on himself. Then the first question a judge asks the accused for a crime against humanity will not be: "Do you plead guilty of crimes with which you are charged?"

So, what would be the right question?

"Will you feel spiritually fulfilled in the event it is confirmed that you were involved in the meaningless activity ascribed to you?"

The future course of proceedings should not depend on that answer. The level of a prosecutor's success would not be measured by a guilty verdict or length of the sentence. The prosecutor would succeed at the level to which the accused pleaded guilty and exposed the distorted psychology that led

to the crime.

Even a prisoner who serves a life sentence might embrace the sentence as his sacrifice, his destiny, and encourage criminal intent among his supporters. Be sure that it is better to have a free-living former predator who has become conscious. He will witness to himself and everyone else about the misconceptions that drove his crimes. The point of criminal justice should not be severe punishment but true spiritual and psychological nurturing of the accused.

And does that mean that all legal proceedings conducted that way would succeed? To me it seems like a medical and psychological procedure rather than a legal approach.

The process might not guarantee general success. But such an approach would reveal how far the voice of reason and justice has influenced the accused. You would be surprised to know that many so-called criminals privately repent actions they are publicly attacked for. Revealing that would be a comprehensive way to eradicate the impulse to hate or act badly. The repentant criminal would be your real success. I don't see much done to achieve it so far.

I don't see anything done in order to achieve it. When criminals are sentenced to forty and more years of prison for what they did, I never see repentance on their faces. I have a feeling that all these people would do the same things again if given an opportunity.

Correct. And remember that punishment does not erase the murderers' impulse to commit terrible crimes. Punishment pushes them deeper into the trackless areas of their minds. Judicial decisions should not result in that. It is not a satisfaction good enough for the victims of crimes. Crime victims know that best of all. A crime victim would take multiplied satisfaction from findings that removed any possible cause for such crimes to be repeated. That's what legal proceedings should strive for. And so should all legal systems.

I am not sure how close or far we are from following the path toward which you are guiding us.

161

That's not up to me. You are the ones mastering your own destinies. By changing yourselves, you will do the most to change your environment. By making a meaningful change in yourself, you will create a more meaningful environment in which to live.

That's correct. But what if someone insists to his very last breath that his old, reactive way of thinking and acting is justified? And he does so where he will never come under any legal jurisdiction?

There is no need for someone to be under a constituted jurisdiction before a new path can open him to enlightenment.

Good. But what if someone keeps insisting on criminal behavior?

All the time? To his last breath in his current human form?

Yes.

Then, that person failed to fulfill the purpose of his life in human form. Then that person opened up other dimensions for his future in the material world.

It's time to speak about karma and reincarnation, about different types of bodily shapes residing on your planet. It's time to identify new topics.

Is that the precisely defined topic you would like to deal with in the rest of the book?

Yes. Even though you haven't asked questions about certain topics, I think you should deal with them. Life after life, a soul's transition into a new body after leaving the previous one. The point of reincarnation. The so-called prize and so-called punishment after death. Birth, life, death. These are all topics that something should be said about. It is important to know how things stand after death in order to take a more appropriate stance in life.

Yes. But at least three of the largest religions in the world do not recognize karma and reincarnation. A huge number of people around the world follow the doctrines of their own religions and do not believe in the reincarnated processes.

A number of philosophic schools deal with karma and

reincarnation, by recognizing them as such. Nevertheless, they do not have a clear vision of what these two notions really mean.

And now, through this book and me you will tell the whole truth to the lost world. Come on! I don't have a sufficiently high opinion of myself to address people that way.

If I paid attention to your opinion of yourself, we would never have started this book. However, I have a plan for you. I have a plan for many well-intentioned and innocent people who will be dealing with this important document.

You are all worthy of everything. You all come from the Supreme and you will remain as such through eternity. Each of you can make the final truth public to the entire world. You are revealing sealed secrets. You are travelers treading through the worst labyrinths. No exit will elude you. There is no trap that you can fall into. Therefore, why do you suppose that, together with me, you cannot declare the truth?

The truth is difficult for most people to grasp, at least at the moment. Even priests in some religions forbid belief in karma and reincarnation. Others confirm those beliefs and add speculations of their own. They all act with the same goal: To strengthen religious and secular authority. It is all about that. Now we are going to proclaim the real meaning of karma and reincarnation, and of course, describe how these two natural phenomena work.

All right. What is the most important point to emphasize, or in other words, which part of this system has been unknown up to now?

As you usually do with sensitive natural phenomena, you have made this one a taboo. You have imagined diverse horrors about what awaits us in the future—hell, eternal fire, devils, purgatory, a violent transition to lower forms of life.

Do you want to say that none of it is true?

I would like to say that it is you, and no one else but you, who decides your future location. You and no one but you.

That means hell *does* exist and each of us will choose whether to abide in eternal fire or not after death. Then there is no one in hell. I don't believe someone would choose a more difficult life, choose punishment for his crimes, if the choice were his.

First of all, it is important to clarify the notion of hell. If you think of a place in the universe created by an avenging god, a place with eternal fire, cauldrons, devils, and all the accompanying elements, then you are surely speculating far off the something we call a limited time of suffering.

Is what we think of as hell related to this "limited time of suffering?"

Yes. Except the hell you describe in your Holy books, and the way you have imagined it doesn't really exist. But suffering does. Every one of you has experienced suffering, or in other words, a limited time of suffering. And you can easily connect the meaning of hell with the meaning of suffering. Suffering is hell. Hell is suffering. Suffering is an unmistakable sign that you need to change something in your life. And that is the point of suffering—a point that should be useful to you. Everyone who suffers in any way experiences a type of hell. This whole book comes to you as advice about how to avoid suffering, how to avoid hell. Use it.

Do you mean that there is hell both in this life and in the life after it?

There is no "this life" and "life after." When you say "life after death," you don't say it in the right way. Life never stops; it continues. Death is not the end of life. Dying is not an abyss taking you to the sphere of nothingness. Life is indestructible, unchangeable, continuous, and eternal. Therefore, there is no "hell before this life" or "hell after life." There is suffering, or in other words there is a limited time of suffering. The process has a purpose.

People know how to overcome a limited time of suffering. Suffering is not a punishment, certainly not my punishing you. Suffering is a sign that something should be changed in your life. When you change, suffering automatically ceases to exist because any continuation of it would be pointless.

Nothing in my world is useless. Everything is bursting with sense and order. There wouldn't be anything more pointless than a hell where your stay would be, for some reason, eternal. Priests who teach such theological misconceptions have, as a rule, already chosen eternal paradise for themselves, not eternal hell. For them, it would be a too embarrassing experience. But they wouldn't object if that experience were assigned to someone else, especially if it were a person who threatens to undermine their own religious pillars. You see, in the world you created, religion puts the power and means to manage people in the hands of only certain people.

Religion is one of the pillars of inappropriate power in this world. Not a single religion is a path toward me.

I have to tell you this: You are a legend. A living legend. Guys, I have to say this aloud: GOD IS A WOMAN AND THAT WOMAN IS A LEGEND.

Ha ha ha ha. We will see what you'll be saying when this book puts temptations in your way.

Fuck. Now I feel as if you are threatening me. You know that I am not so brave. You are hampering my intentions.

Great. Now I made you swear—and on purpose. I haven't closed the topic of "purposefulness swearing" yet.

I remember. You scolded me earlier for swearing …

I do not scold people. I do not punish them. Even though I am your teacher, I will not send you to the naughty corner because you used an inappropriate word. In any case, you used that swearword appropriately just now.

What kind of God are you? First you say that you haven't created eternal suffering, and now you approve of swearing at you yourself—at God.

When swearing is a symbol of love, instead of hatred and powerlessness, then it is a good swearword. So it is that the swearword took its place in the world I created. In intimate love relations between me and you, me and any of you, swearing is a funny way of showing affection. Haven't you

ever sworn at your child or your lover in an attempt to love and not to offend and insult people?

I have. And that is good. That is really a part of the completeness of everything. You said, "I am guiding you toward being complete in everything. Be brave and open enough to stop suffering and the state of hell. Go toward happiness, enjoyment, and completeness. Thus, all things will have meaning and purpose including hell, love, and swearwords."

Protection

You still make me worry. Twice you've told me I might have problems because of this book. Of course, that's not going to prevent me from making it public to the whole world. Nevertheless, I'm uneasy about the consequences.

Don't worry. You will be under my protection. You will have my protection all the time.

Is there anyone who is not under your protection?

A good question. Of course, everyone is under my protection, but only up to the moment when someone decides to go out from under my wing. Thus, that person starts a reactive life. A life of illusion. Anyone who tries to interrupt this book's publication or prevent spreading its messages is leading a reactive life. Not creative, a reactive life.

But it is no reason for someone to be condemned. How can one find out all the benefits of a creative life unless he experiences a reactive life at some point?

Exactly. Wonderful.

Also, how can one be aware of the fantastic character of living under your wing, without having the opposite experience?

Nice. Very nice. No condemnation, no value judgment, no cursing, and no guilt.

Now do I understand what Jesus meant by "if someone slaps your left cheek, also give him your right one?"

With this in mind, Jesus kept saying, "Father, forgive them, because they don't know what they're doing!" Even though he was crucified, Jesus was under my protection at all times.

To be honest, I wouldn't like to experience that exact form of your protection.

You don't understand what I am talking about when I talk about Jesus and his crucifixion. You are not aware what form of my protection Jesus received.

And in the end he looked up and said: "Father, why did you leave me?"

And thus he ended the dark night of the soul's final phase. After that, nothing was the same for Jesus. I opened up the entire world to him. The entire world with its fantastic character. He experienced something that, in your limited knowledge of what really happened to him, you call "resurrection."

What really happened to Jesus?

He became a spiritual, creative being full of knowledge, love, happiness, and blissfulness. He became like me.

And for that reason, many consider Jesus to be God?

Yes. And now we are going to stop that dilemma.
    JESUS BECAME GOD, NOT TO REPLACE ME OR PUT HIMSELF ON A COSMIC PEDESTAL, BUT TO TEACH YOU THAT YOU ALL CAN BECOME GODS.
    WHEN YOU LIVE LIFE WITH GOD, THEN YOU LIVE THE LIFE OF GOD.
    AND I AM THE ONLY GOD OF ALL OF YOU.

Hmm. Quite inspirational. So now I can proclaim that Jesus wasn't God, but he taught all of us how to become Gods.

Of course. As a matter of fact, Jesus, was neither better nor worse than any of you individually. Neither were other prophets, gurus, teachers, or masters. To understand and

accept this truth will make you truly powerful. In such a way you will remember the repeated application of power that is inherent in you. It is the way to wake up, come to your senses, and achieve productive humility.

Productive humility?

Yes. The point of humility is not to swallow your pride before an individual, an institution, or a god. To be humble means to be aware that you have all power and abilities in you yourselves. When you fully understand that, there will be no need to prove yourself to anyone or anything, to fight or show off, to protest or express displeasure, to ask or beg. People who seem to be in a better position than you, and those who would be predators toward you, will pose no danger at all.

The only thing you would wish at the critical instance would be for the person trying to hurt you to understand how his way of life and thinking are limited. You will wish that he didn't underestimate himself and his abilities, that he weren't on the path of darkness and indecision, and that he weren't acting contrary to his untouched but limitless mental and spiritual potential. For that reason, Jesus begged of his "Father, forgive them. They don't know what they're doing" as he was crucified.

Interesting. It is especially interesting to hear your simple explanation of truths that have been unclear and vague until now. I will try to banish fear of unpleasant events that might occur after this book is published.

Don't worry. You are under my protection. You are all under my protection. The only condition for living in perfect safety is your becoming aware of my protection and allowing it to become one of the key factors in your life.

New forms of awareness will be the most difficult task you set for us.

I have never given you a task. You ask and I respond. Many pray for a message from me, and this book is one of the messages I send. You have asked for it. Deep in your heart you have felt that you could become taller, stronger, and

more powerful than ever. Now get up and say publicly that a time of awareness and renaissance has come. Now is the time to understand suffering and transform it into enjoyment and meaningful living as you have been striving to do. Be officials, workers, or farmers, students, teachers, engineers, technicians, craftsmen, laborers, poets, writers, musicians, journalists, or painters. Be what you are or what you are yet to become, but be it wholeheartedly and with all your potential. Act as spiritual and creative beings in every work, activity, or creation and you will create the world of purposefulness, harmony, and integration.

But what if someone keeps insisting on violence and malevolence toward fellow creatures? What if someone simply doesn't accept the model of the world you propose?

Then during his life as a human, that person will fail to fulfill the purpose he picked for himself even before he was born in his body. The human form of life has its own purpose. The point of living for any of you is to live, but not with hatred, insecurity, greed, estrangement, and egocentrism. That is not what you intended for yourself before you were born. If you insist on useless procedures and outcomes, then your next body will not be human, and you yourself will choose that body.

How? Why would we deliberately choose a position that would be unpleasant? I think that most people would avoid such a decision, if possible.

After death, especially after death, you enter living spheres that don't have much in common with all you noticed and felt in the previous body. The universe is a highly sophisticated mechanism through which you are trying to achieve the purpose of existence. Intergalactic expanses, stars, pulsars, black holes, galaxies, and nebulae exist for it, for him, and for you. There is not a single part of endless creation that you are not related to in a special way. You are all parts of a large whole.

Nevertheless, you are all separate individuals. You are Singlediverse. You live and die to live and die again. But the

point is to stop death, dying, and uncertainty. The aim is to get out of the cosmic wheel of birth and death. The fact that you have to be born again simply means that there is something to be done on your self. Each new birth begins with a new task that you set. After death in the spatial and time continuum, your perception of space and time and self changes significantly. You sense the narrow meaning of time on Earth when you were limited by your body-mind and senses.

After death, mind and senses transcend. Intelligence takes the place it deserves, while the soul rises above all components as leader in the existential way of thinking. That is a new world. That is what you really are, distilled and more intense than before death. Then a complete profile of your past life opens up to you and you are peacefully and blissfully aware of its good and bad aspects. You know what is good and what is not in all you had been engaged in. You know what was close to you yourself while you were active on the Earth—and what was not. You know it all, as the time for knowing has come.

Then don't exult over others, and don't lament either. Don't scream for joy, but don't sorrow either. You know perfectly well what step will take you closer to what you really are. You see what distanced you from yourself or brought you closer during your previous incarnation.

That next step will be to quickly, insightfully identify the sensibility you strive for. Those parameters and measures will be exact. There is no room for calculations and speculations. There is no gap between thinking and acting. It's all true, because truth is all you are made of. That is a time of decision making, and each of your decisions after deaths, when you choose the way your life will continue, will be the best decision. You know perfectly well what you have to lose in order to get, and what you have to get in order to lose, what you have to lose in order to lose, and what you have to get in order to get.

And then, with complete understanding and knowledge of what you have achieved and how far you have come in your return to me/yourself, each of you decides which body to settle in next, or more precisely, which material body your spiritual entity will focus on—you are not in bodies, you are around and focused on them. And that next body can be the body of an amoeba or God, or some other body, one out of billions of types that you currently know or don't know about, that are currently inhabiting or not inhabiting the planet on which you live. The decision is all yours. Any decision you make at such a high level of life awareness (and you always achieve it after you leave a material body) will be the one that is timely, at the right place, and at the proper center of conscious reasoning.

And we will not deliberately avoid the unpleasant options?

No. Since anything that takes you back to sense will be ennobling. It will not diminish you, even if you go to the start of the evolution chain for a bodily form. You will choose the path of understanding and knowledge and finally leaving samsara, the cosmic circle of birth and death.

After breaking chains of birth and death, those souls come back to you.

Yes. As they return to themselves. And not only certain souls. All of you will return.

And you are in the hearts of all of us.

Yes. As I am in endless spiritual worlds.

Once we return to you, we will never end up again in the material world.

There will be no need for it, as you will know and feel then that you have understood the illusion of relativity and can fully realize the absolute world. You will have the necessary understanding. You will be satisfied and self-sacrificing. You will be in everything, and everything will be in you. There will be nothing unknown to you and more and more new information will come to you in eternity.

What relation will we/I have with you in the world of the absolute?

A relation full of love, passion, and refined lust. In the world and relation you would return to, nothing can be missing. Nothing will be missing either in you or me. Here where I am, and with me, there is no illness, powerlessness, weakness, grievance, or envy. We have it all, and everything and everyone will be able to have us. In my world, there is no headache, backache, old age, ugliness, or depression. Everything is in constant and excited movement. Each movement is a dance, each sound is a song.

Will we have a Singlediverse character there, too?

Truth is truth, be it in the material or spiritual empire. Truth, like light, spreads in all directions infinitely. Lies are the mind's fabrication. Illusions are the source of lies. Your powerlessness and anger arise from purposeless action under the wing of illusion. Further, suffering and weakness are reminders that something important in your understanding of your life should be changed. If you want to change behavior, you have to change the way you understand things first. Changing behavior precedes changing reactions. Soon, your life path will be creative instead of reactive and it will be the path leading to me, and to the world of my absolute. Light will burst out in all directions at unimaginable speed.

Once … once you said you were my wife.

In our ultimate relation, I am your girlfriend.

I don't know what to say.

Perhaps you could sing.

Are you referring to the song that keeps coming back to my mind?

This is the line I brought up from your long-term memory.

"Hey, crazy head, that's what you're doing to me,

what will I do with it, where should I go?

on the road without end?"[23]

---

23   Branimir Štulić, Želja.

And I Have a Guarantee for You

Truth be told, I don't know what I should do or how to behave on this path with no end. You silly …

Follow your intuition. When you have to choose between reason and intuition, choose intuition. When you have to choose between reason and superstition, choose reason. Intuition is not based on superstition. It immediately separates from superstition by way of reason. The logic of reason should be given priority over the senseless reactions of superstition. Belief in me is both intuitive and rational. Belief in what is not borders on superstition. Superstition is fear of what is not.

And I am not yet clear about who I am and what my final relation with you may be, regardless of the fact that you so engagingly gave me a hint about who you are—may God forgive me—my girl. I may sound as if I am going round in circles, but I am still at the same place where I always have been.

For each of you, I can be anyone and anything as long as our mutual relationship is based on love, knowledge, blissfulness, or happiness. You are no exception, either in a positive or negative context. Nobody can be an exception, as between you and me there is no designation or category. Therefore, why can't I be your girlfriend, or the girlfriend of any other spiritual individual? All relations that you mutually establish in the material world are only distorted reflections of the complete relationship we have in realm of the absolute.

The material world is a distorted reflection of the empire of the absolute. Many of you believe that the world of God is unvaried and uninteresting. That is wrong. My world is the world of diversity, mysteries, and adventure. All perfect things in the material world also exist in spiritual dimensions close to me. Come to me, and turn to transcendentally complete living. My world is the world of expansion of miracles and the ultimate magic. An adventure is about to start ...

I hope I will not fall short of your call.

No, you will not. Neither you nor anyone else.

You taught me never to resort to violence.

Yes. I reminded you of the knowledge you possess.

But, if I wanted to join you, I would have to fight my own lethargy.

It is correct that I have advised you to avoid fighting. But fighting is not the same as dedication, putting in an effort or encouraging one's will.

Please explain.

Very gladly. I will try to explain it to you in a short and simple way. Fighting is a sign of powerlessness. You already understood that much. But dedication and effort reflect one's will. Don't fight your own lethargy, as you describe it. Encourage will and dedication to leave the world of stagnation and turn to the world of activity, a healthy turn. It can be a lifestyle. You have been spending days in inactivity and overeating. You think I don't see it, and that I will not mention it. I was just waiting for the right time to tell you what I think about it ...

Now you have just started behaving like a peevish girl ....

Not peevish, caring. I care about you and I kind of feel that you would like me to personally care about you. Am I right?

You are right. Say what you have to say.

I want to tell you to stop useless fighting—against shortage finances, illness, obesity, and fighting in fear and with fear. It is time for you to stop it all. Encourage your will and aspiration for healthy activity. Don't burden yourself with the past, as the burden of past events will cause those events to repeat. Don't worry about the future. Focus on the present. Both past and future, each of them in its own way, spill over into present. Once you manage to fix the present, demons of the past and future will cease to exist.

Please. Can you tell me concretely what to do next and how to do it, how to treat myself in my daily routine?

Of course I will tell you more about it and more concretely. First, cut your food intake. Now you weigh 115 kg and have set your weight goal at 105, after that at 95 kg. Realistically speaking, and having in mind your metabolism and eating habits, you can achieve it in four to six months. To help you out with this I suggest you reduce your food intake to the very least one day in a week and also to take nothing but water once a week. Only once a week indulge in an unhealthy food you crave. Thus nutrition will become meaningful to you and your body. Exercise more, eat less, and spend less time watching TV. Engage in some physical activity at least five times a week. Sport for your body is what yoga is for your mind. Having in mind your body type, I would suggest you engage in two basic activities that you can practice at any time of the year— cycling and walking. Buy a stationary bike for indoor exercise in bad weather. Go out and take a walk whenever you can and want to. You already know how pleasant and inspiring it can be. With the passage of time, when you get in shape, join groups of people who enjoy hiking. Thus, you will find the advantages of close contact with nature. You already are devoted to preservation of natural resources. Nature will pay you back in a number of ways.

So much for losing weight and getting into shape. How should I deal with money shortage and fears about that? I know that you were speaking generally and conceptually about these problems, but tell me concretely what to do in my daily routine.

All I said generally applies specifically to your situation and also to everyone else's. I'll advise you in detail about your case, but everything I am about to say can be useful to anyone who is working through this book.

Review your top priorities, as you have already determined them. What remains is to stick to them with your body and will. You seem to be doing so, more and more. You have accepted quite a lot of the philosophy and approaches to life that we have discussed in this book. Material advancement is already approaching. There remains quite a lot in order to close the perfect circle. Don't set any deadlines for yourself. To achieve life perfection is not the same as losing fifteen or twenty kg. But it isn't all that much different either. As a matter of fact, the technique of achieving success is the same in every instance: Transform hope and belief into certainty that the goal you've set will be achieved. The further the goal is, or seems to be, the more difficult it is to your understanding about how to reach it.

Add two more components to this working model: Feel gratitude to me for current or imminent advances toward a particular ideal. And adopt or activate work as the mode to achievement.

Everyone must define his or her own work mode to stop enhance income and escape the money shortage. Work is good for all as long as it doesn't hurt or deprive anyone. Muslims call it halal work, and money made that way is considered halal money.[24] Only halal—beneficial—work is part of active prayer, which is always good to rely on. You can't be dealing drugs and still expect your work to be part of active prayer. You can't be a contract killer—unscrupulous butcher, manufacturer of weapons of mass destruction, or a military authority ordering executions—and still be engaged in active prayer. In order to help others toward fulfillment of their desires, your work must not be to the detriment or at the expense of anyone else.

Your priority work is your writing, and that is a good choice. Everyone should make his or her choice and the possibilities are endless. It is more purposeful to be an uneducated but honest street cleaner than a highly educated

---

24   Halal—approved of, beneficial, Arabic.

general ordering murder and destruction. A street cleaner is one of those great professions that you work at with your active prayer. You can pray as a housewife, bricklayer, painter, plumber, driver, electrician, information technician, engineer, university professor, or chimney sweeper. You may be a laborer, farmer, or artist, and through all these types of work, you may activate your active prayer.

The possibilities are endless indeed. Purposeful decisions bring about positive reactions. The knowledge that everything will be just fine makes things happen. A thought is creative.

As for you personally, as you finance yourself through trade and services you perform, you can expect a bingo in your writing. You know it yourself: Through writing you manage to express yourself in the best possible way—better than through some other activities you have been involved in, even though each of them might fulfill the purpose of what it is you seek for yourself and your world.

Does it mean that it is better to avoid performing several duties at the same time?

You can do as many things at the same time as you can manage, and you should do them in such a way that neither you nor others are burdened. Your era opens up a number of business and creative possibilities, many more than were available in the past several thousands of years. At the same time, your dependence on technology and resources leave you feeling more and more alienated from one another. Anyone can see for himself that mutual distance and isolation from other people and other species lead you to personal alienation.

When you are alienated from each other, then you alienate yourself from yourself, as well and vice versa. It confirms your singlediverse nature. Insisting on staying close only to people of one class, race, ethnicity, religion, or political affiliation, at the cost of distancing yourself from different people (those you consider of lower value than yourself), will make you uncomfortable. You will be constantly fighting; you will be exposed to uncertainty and tension.

Soon you will realize that the condition is not natural. You are not here to fight. Your destiny is to develop and achieve

self-realization. The more you manage to do it, the more you will have a positive influence on your surroundings— immediate and distant. Then the closer and clearer the paths of other self-realized individuals will be to you. At the same time, the way toward spiritual knowledge will not appear to be the same for everyone. Your diversity will be the wealth that funds and protects you. Diversity will no longer be a factor in deadly clashes and destabilization—pointless practices rife throughout the entire world.

I absolutely agree. Nicely said. We live in the ignorant world, but it seems to me that this book, thanks to you, offers wisdom and buoyant inspiration. However, I am running out of inspiration.

I have dealt with most of the most pressing issues and feel it's time to close. Working on this book is the key factor in some existential and metaphysical changes—as well as changes in my immediate circumstance. Yet, I don't know how to finish at the same level on which I started. I find it difficult to express myself now or say how I feel as my life changes.

Many of your messages arrived in bottles. Many bottles were broken.

Of course, this is not the end of my research on that fantastic phenomenon of relationship with God. I would be more than glad if any form of this text helped anyone at any time to develop that relationship, which is of crucial importance to each of us. I and so many people, regardless of where we come from, have simply lost that relationship. What causes such loss? If we put aside the philosophical notion that understanding one extreme leads to understanding its opposite, then it is obvious that many other causes interrupt the essential relation we should have with God. And as obviously, that relation is experiencing a crisis. Mankind is struggling with hatred, destructive envy, unproductive insecurity, empty claims, intolerance (religious, racial, gender, and ethnic). I think that this book responds to challenges ahead. The readers meet us as individuals and as intelligent beings grouped on this planet. We are all One but are still diverse.

Ideas of Singlediversity came to me for the first time when I was working on this book. I had never heard of it before, so I looked up the word in every encyclopedia and dictionary I could find. Now I conclude that the term Singlediversity is original, presented for the first time in this book, in as specific and engaging manner as I can express it.

If only one person uses these ideas to identify the meaning of his existence and actions, I will be happy and satisfied. My hopes of course, go beyond that, that one person finds his way following guidelines from this book, *God Is a Woman*. In my wildest dreams, I hope that many more, even entire groups of people, will focus on work that will make this world a better, richer place to live than it has been so far. As an outcome, that wouldn't be bad at all. It would be fantastic.

I hope that many will share with me their dreams for realizing this vision. I hope our next dream will avoid the monotonous intolerance and sameness that so often accompany preaching on Oneness and Diversity. You don't have to agree with every statement in this book in order to fit into a Holy process together with others. We are not looking for like-minded people, but well-intentioned ones. We do not aspire to make a society of blindly devoted members. Our paradise will be made of free, spiritual, creative individuals.

Would you be against such a world?

Ask yourselves and then say "No." Be confident that you will achieve your well-intentioned goal. Start working toward it.

And look for your God at the same time. God will certainly come to you as in this Holy moment he/she/it has no more loved or more important work to do.

I guarantee it.

Yours truly,
   Edin Husković
   edhuskovic@gmail.com

About the Author

Author Edin Husković was born in Mostar in 1973 in Bosnia and Herzegovina. He has published five books so far:

1. Opet Strah (Fear Again), Prva književna komuna, First literary commune, Mostar, 1991, poetry.
2. Pustinjak (Hermit), Edicija Rondo, Rondo edition, Mostar, 1996, a collection of fragmentary prose.
3. Istok, Balkan, Zapad (East, Balkan, West), Slovo, Letter, Mostar, 2000, a collection of stories.
4. Dnevnik iz Utrobe (Diary from the bowels), Zigo, Rijeka, Croatia, 2007, a novel reviewed by Predrag Matvejević, the most translated writer from former Yugoslavia in the world.
5. Poslanica Južnim Slavenima (God is a Woman), the publisher in Bosnia and Herzegovina is the Center for Critical Thought, and the publisher for the English-speaking area is Ozark Mountain Publishing, 2023.

He is an author of the column at „Tačno"(Exactly) Internet portal (www.tacno.net), where he publishes underground stories together with the most renowned authors from the area of the former Yugoslavia.

He lives and works in Mostar, Bosnia and Herzegovina.

Other Books by Ozark Mountain Publishing, Inc.

Dolores Cannon
A Soul Remembers Hiroshima
Between Death and Life
Conversations with Nostradamus,
    Volume I, II, III
The Convoluted Universe -Book One,
    Two, Three, Four, Five
The Custodians
Five Lives Remembered
Horns of the Goddess
Jesus and the Essenes
Keepers of the Garden
Legacy from the Stars
The Legend of Starcrash
The Search for Hidden Sacred
    Knowledge
They Walked with Jesus
The Three Waves of Volunteers and the
    New Earth
A Very Special Friend
Aron Abrahamsen
Holiday in Heaven
James Ream Adams
Little Steps
Justine Alessi & M. E. McMillan
Rebirth of the Oracle
Kathryn Andries
Time: The Second Secret
Will Alexander
Call Me Jonah
Cat Baldwin
Divine Gifts of Healing
The Forgiveness Workshop
Penny Barron
The Oracle of UR
P.E. Berg & Amanda Hemmingsen
The Birthmark Scar
Dan Bird
Finding Your Way in the Spiritual Age
Waking Up in the Spiritual Age
Julia Cannon
Soul Speak – The Language of Your
    Body
Jack Cauley
Journey for Life
Ronald Chapman
Seeing True
Jack Churchward
Lifting the Veil on the Lost
    Continent of Mu

The Stone Tablets of Mu
Carolyn Greer Daly
Opening to Fullness of Spirit
Patrick De Haan
The Alien Handbook
Paulinne Delcour-Min
Divine Fire
Holly Ice
Spiritual Gold
Anthony DeNino
The Power of Giving and Gratitude
Joanne DiMaggio
Edgar Cayce and the Unfulfilled
    Destiny of Thomas Jefferson
Reborn
Paul Fisher
Like a River to the Sea
Anita Holmes
Twidders
Aaron Hoopes
Reconnecting to the Earth
Edin Huskovic
God is a Woman
Patricia Irvine
In Light and In Shade
Kevin Killen
Ghosts and Me
Susan Linville
Blessings from Agnes
Donna Lynn
From Fear to Love
Curt Melliger
Heaven Here on Earth
Where the Weeds Grow
Henry Michaelson
And Jesus Said – A Conversation
Andy Myers
Not Your Average Angel Book
Holly Nadler
The Hobo Diaries
Guy Needler
The Anne Dialogues
Avoiding Karma
Beyond the Source – Book 1, Book 2
The Curators
The History of God
The OM
The Origin Speaks

For more information about any of the above titles, soon to be released titles,
or other items in our catalog, write, phone or visit our website:
PO Box 754, Huntsville, AR 72740|479-738-2348/800-935-0045|www.ozarkmt.com

Other Books by Ozark Mountain Publishing, Inc.

Psycho Spiritual Healing
James Nussbaumer
And Then I Knew My Abundance
Each of You
Living Your Dram, Not Someone Else's
The Master of Everything
Mastering Your Own Spiritual Freedom
Sherry O'Brian
Peaks and Valley's
Gabrielle Orr
Akashic Records: One True Love
Let Miracles Happen
Nikki Pattillo
Children of the Stars
A Golden Compass
Victoria Pendragon
Being In A Body
Sleep Magic
The Sleeping Phoenix
Alexander Quinn
Starseeds What's It All About
Debra Rayburn
Let's Get Natural with Herbs
Charmian Redwood
A New Earth Rising
Coming Home to Lemuria
Richard Rowe
Exploring the Divine Library
Imagining the Unimaginable
Garnet Schulhauser
Dance of Eternal Rapture
Dance of Heavenly Bliss
Dancing Forever with Spirit
Dancing on a Stamp
Dancing with Angels in Heaven
Annie Stillwater Gray
The Dawn Book
Education of a Guardian Angel
Joys of a Guardian Angel
Work of a Guardian Angel
Manuella Stoerzer
Headless Chicken

Blair Styra
Don't Change the Channel
Who Catharted
Natalie Sudman
Application of Impossible Things
L.R. Sumpter
Judy's Story
The Old is New
We Are the Creators
Artur Tradevosyan
Croton
Croton II
Jim Thomas
Tales from the Trance
Jolene and Jason Tierney
A Quest of Transcendence
Paul Travers
Dancing with the Mountains
Nicholas Vesey
Living the Life-Force
Dennis Wheatley/ Maria Wheatley
The Essential Dowsing Guide
Maria Wheatley
Druidic Soul Star Astrology
Sherry Wilde
The Forgotten Promise
Lyn Willmott
A Small Book of Comfort
Beyond all Boundaries Book 1
Beyond all Boundaries Book 2
Beyond all Boundaries Book 3
D. Arthur Wilson
You Selfish Bastard
Stuart Wilson & Joanna Prentis
Atlantis and the New Consciousness
Beyond Limitations
The Essenes -Children of the Light
The Magdalene Version
Power of the Magdalene
Sally Wolf
Life of a Military Psychologist

For more information about any of the above titles, soon to be released titles,
or other items in our catalog, write, phone or visit our website:
PO Box 754, Huntsville, AR 72740|479-738-2348/800-935-0045|www.ozarkmt.com